OUT OF DENIAL
Piecing Together a Fractured Life

BY ROBERT K. ANDERSON

Lulu.com
2008

Author's note: This is a much revised version of a book
informally self-published in 2005 as *Testament of Denial* (60
copies, spiral-bound, no ISBN).

ISBN: 978-1-4357-2061-9

*This book is dedicated to the memory of
my mother and father
MARION and ROBERT ANDERSON*

*and to the emerging presence of
CRAZY BOB
who has taken a long time
coming into his own.*

CONTENTS

HOME FREE

COMING OUT

GIFTS

Foreword

The soul has its own history. It is mostly hidden, glimpsed at the margins, hinted in highlight and shadow, guessed through dream and memory. We can tell our stories, we can think we live them, bristling with an array of intentions, explanations and excuses, but the truth is, our stories tell us, they tell us who we are, deep down, at the core.

Memory is a heroic act. To try to remember enough of one's life, to see it steady and whole, discerning the basic connections, the patterns and motifs that give it shape and meaning, is to try to stand still in the whirlwind of time and put one's finger to the truth. Has one gone deep enough to catch the essence?

For years I denied a basic truth about myself, that I was gay, yet for all the distortion and the damage that was done, what I see in the pattern of my life is an amazing generosity, a repeated invitation to step into the fullness of my being, whatever my resistance. Lessons and opportunities were offered again and again, the rhythm of renewal never ceased, and dream and memory preserved intact essential information for use years later in healing, when I was finally ready to own who I was.

Generosity – one might almost call it grace. Some people talk of the need to save their souls. My soul saved me. This book is the story of that rescue.

–Robert K. Anderson
MINNEAPOLIS, MINNESOTA, JUNE 2008

IN RETROSPECT

A Leap, a Look Back

I came out in my late thirties after sixteen years of marriage, and I came out like gangbusters. I told anyone who would listen, even strangers at the bus stop. I'd tell friends I hadn't seen in years, in casual conversation or over the phone – "Oh, by the way..." I could squeeze the information into almost any situation, like a 60-second public service announcement. I spared only the aged and infirm: my 96-year-old grandfather who had just entered a nursing home, and my 80-year-old great aunt who was dying from emphysema. I'm surprised I showed that much restraint.

Coming out was an eruption of expressive free-dom for me, a one-man Renaissance. A secret so horrible I had dared tell no one for years was finally out in the open at last. To understand the energy behind this, you need to know two things about me. I grew up in the repressive, sanitized Fifties, before the liberation heyday of the late Sixties, and like many gay boys who compensate for their sense of shame by being too perfect in every respect, I took the rules and values of that conformist culture too much to heart.

Within a few weeks of deciding to come out in 1980, however, I had told my parents, my 10-year-old daughter, all my friends and my colleagues at work. I didn't even care if my supervisor found out. It wasn't exactly a decision any more. I simply had to tell. The pressure from a lifetime of shame and secrecy had built to the bursting point.

I'm not particularly proud of how I did it. I was careless of other people's feelings, of their need to receive the information in a context that would help them deal with it. I told my daughter at the same time she learned Judy and I were divorcing, as I was putting her to bed one night after a visit to Grandma and Grandpa's. She cried at the news of the divorce, then laughed when I told her I was gay. She quickly reached out to touch my arm.

"I'm sorry, Dad, but it just sounds funny – I mean, it's so weird," she said. And then came the inevitable question: "What do two men do, anyway?" Like too many kids these days, Rachel was precocious, grown-up beyond her years, and more brave than any kid should have to be. I'm least proud of how I told her; I put little thought into what and when and how.

I know men who have agonized over these questions. One friend discussed with a support group for a year the decision of when to tell his teenage son, then decided to wait until the boy was safely through adolescence; his younger son, who was somewhat homophobic, he chose not to tell till he was in his late twenties. These questions of timing are always dicey, and can be answered in many different ways. Let the record show, I didn't hesitate, not for a minute.

I rationalized: I've dealt with this problem my entire life, carried the whole weight of it by myself. It's taken its toll in paralysis and depression. Let others deal with it for a change.

And I let go. As simple as that. I let go of a lifetime of deceiving myself and others, of denying and compartmentalizing my feelings, of pretending and playing roles and being phony with the people I loved most. I had lived a lie – no more!

Beyond my impulsiveness and insensitivity, in some sense redeeming them, lay a new-found *joie de vivre*, a hunger for the truth, and a need to be made whole. It was as simple as that.

When I came out, more than twenty years ago now, a friend of mine, a cartoonist and a lesbian, drew a card for me. On the cover is a closet door, open just a crack, with two eyes peering out of the darkness, anxious and cowering near the floor. On the inside, the door is flung open and the figure has sprung out into the light, head thrown back, hair standing on end with excitement, arms flung open to the world in ecstasy, propelled into the present as if through the uncoiling of a giant spring.

I want to say, after I came out, I never looked back. And in one sense, that's true. I have met this experience with open arms. I have no regrets about this odyssey of discovery. It has proved a source of renewal and energy that infuses itself to this day into every corner of my life. My creativity, my capacity for friendship, my willingness to embark on new adventures, to push limits and test myself, my spirituality – all take their energy from here, this radical declaration of freedom and independence. It isn't that I don't have problems any more. I'm going blind, I'm aging, I still struggle with issues of intimacy, empathy, social responsibility, pride, wrath, sloth, lust, the whole panoply of human ills.

But the difference is, I own these problems, because I own my life. I am not playing out a role according to somebody else's rules and expectations; I am not watching my life unfold around me as if it belonged to somebody else. I choose, I act, I take responsibility, I grow. The struggle has meaning because it is mine.

A friend once said that being married and being gay, for him, was like living inside a glass jar. You saw everything that was happening to you, you went through the motions, but you didn't connect, you weren't fully present. You viewed yourself like a specimen under glass.

One man I knew could not speak of his marriage without weeping. Earl had been married for thirty-five years and was totally faithful to his wife. He loved her and was a dutiful, caring husband and father. She developed cancer and Earl took early retirement to nurse her through the last two years of her life. When she died, he came out at age 65 – hardly prime time to put yourself on the market. Everywhere you went in the gay community – the bars, salons, parties, pot-lucks, card games – there was Earl, intense, lonely, garrulous, usually telling his story to some luckless guy who looked vaguely uneasy, like the wedding guest fingered by the glittery-eyed Ancient Mariner. Loneliness is hardly a strong selling point. If you were really lucky, Earl gave you one of his bone-crunching bear-hugs. But eventually Earl found somebody, a sweet guy thirty years his junior, and they moved to San Diego to set up housekeeping.

Throughout his marriage Earl had behaved honorably; he had no reason to reproach himself. But on at least two occasions I saw him break down when he spoke of his wife and his marriage: "I was false to her... she never knew me for who I really was. I wasn't true, I always kept a part of myself hidden from her. She must have known, and it must have hurt her." His grief was inconsolable.

The grief of in authenticity is a grief many married gay men share. It runs deep and takes many forms. Whether the issue is being true to yourself or another, betraying your own values or someone else's trust, sacrificing an essential part of your sexuality or identity, the grief is immeasurable, because it goes to the core of your being.

I want to say, when I came out, I never looked back. My life, my real life, began then. In a support group I was in at the time, the Gay Fathers' Group, we had a saying: "You've got your chronological age and then you've got your gay age, your real age, which dates from when you came out." We sometimes said this jokingly to excuse adolescent behavior in otherwise mature, responsible men. Group members were professionals and family men in their late-thirties, forties and fifties, some of them divorced and newly out, others committed to staying in their marriage. But coming out did have its wild side, sometimes called the "candy-store" phase: "I'll take one of those and one of those, and that bright red one over there, and some of that gunky-looking stuff on the back shelf." It's funny, and sad too, because there's no way to make up for lost time, no way to recover an adolescence you never had.

When I came out, it was a full, joyous leap into an unknown future. Yet, like Earl and so many other gay married men, I'm haunted. I'm haunted by a marriage that failed, in part, because I passed through it in a daze of denial. I'm haunted by the hurt caused to three people – me, my ex-wife and my daughter – because I was trying so hard to be something I was not. I'm haunted by the part of my life I never lived, by the boy I never knew.

I once dated a priest who must have felt it was part of his pastoral duty to confess me, for he told me one evening as I lapsed into my own Ancient Mariner mode, relating my tale of loss and woe, "I'm sorry to hear that from you, Bob. I fear you won't be right with yourself till you can affirm your marriage as part of your life."

I'm still working on it. Just the other side of this glorious adventure lies the shadow of grief, which gives a keener edge to all its joys and keeps me tethered to my past despite my embrace of an unfolding future.

Karner

I had met Karner many years ago, seen him maybe three or four times one hot summer when we were both sixteen, and now, as he sat somewhere opposite me in the gloom of my mother's house, in a roomful of family, I felt cool and distant. Was I still angry after forty years?

Most of the guests were already seated in the living room when he arrived with my Aunt Virginia and her husband Glenn, Karner's father. Or rather, I assumed he had arrived. My family was lax with the niceties of protocol: no one introduced him, no one in the room said hello, and Karner rose to the occasion by seating himself without saying a word. I was too blind to see in the dim light, but I knew he was coming for dinner that Easter, and I wondered how it would be between us.

I was seated at the dining room table with my mother, just off the living room, in full view of the front door, but the glare from the picture window threw everything in the room into deep shadow, leaving the seated figures looking like draped Victorian furniture in one of those ancient dark daguerreotypes – except occasionally the furniture spoke: "Yeah, teaching's a lot like court-ing...," and I missed the punch line, it was inserted so deftly into the conversation. I heard my sister-in-law Mary's throaty laugh, joined by chuckles of approval from the others.

It was Karner. I couldn't make out his shape, sunk as it was in the high-backed love seat across the room, but I looked in the direction of that voice, weighing for an instant whether to say hello. It had already established itself, however, fitting so naturally into the flow of conversation that my greeting would have seemed superfluous. I listened and laughed with the others.

With those first few words I heard the boy of nearly a lifetime ago: that shy, soft drawl, the gentle, unself-conscious humor, the genial chuckling at his own jokes, delivered with impeccable timing and pitch, all expressed with an easy languor at once relaxed and inviting. In an instant he was back – the handsome, lanky boy of sixteen with his long, intelligent face, those soft, pursed lips, clear blue eyes, and that confident, graceful self-absorption. He had worn no shirt or shoes in that long sultry summer, and looked as if he had been poured into his sleek faded denims. I wasn't struck with his beauty then, but now, in retrospect...

What I felt then, as I paid my visits, was mainly a sense of obligation, and perhaps curiosity about the new kid in town. Karner was visiting his father for the first time since his parents' divorce and his father's move to Robbinsdale to court and marry my aunt, his sweetheart from years back. Virginia wanted Karner's stay to be pleasant, and she thought I could entertain him and introduce him to some of my friends.

I was a dutiful nephew. Two or three times I

trudged the mile and a half from my house to hers, arriving hot and sweaty only to be met with Karner's cool aplomb. In the dim, stuffy interior of my aunt's house, with the shades and curtains drawn against the midday heat – I remembered the scene as if it were yesterday – he sprawled in an overstuffed chair, speaking in that lazy drawl, his lean legs spilling over the broad arm of the chair, his long, tapered feet and toes suspended in air, the same tawny color as his arms and broad-shouldered torso. His tan seemed to insinuate itself even into the paleness between his toes. Some bodies were made for sun, the cling of low-slung Levis, and the comfort of overstuffed chairs. His butch haircut, a soft, thick brush bleached almost blond by the sun, hung low over his forehead. Those bright blue eyes seemed mostly to be looking elsewhere – at some corner of the room, the door to the hallway, the crack in the drapes – as if they might discover there some adventure more enticing than what presented itself here.

Me, in other words. I leaned forward, too earnestly, my elbows on my knees, focused on his every word; I was such a good listener. I asked him questions about himself, about life and school in Everett, Washington, and about his music. Like his father, he was a musician and played trombone in the school band. I was always so good at making other people feel important. Karner didn't need any encouragement.

Eventually that summer, the routine wore thin. He didn't want to do anything but stay cool and dry in my aunt's house. And one day, when we had agreed to meet some of my friends at a local hamburger joint to play pinball, and I had walked the dutiful distance under an unrelenting sun, and he met me at the door with his usual indifference, smiling and saying he had forgotten all about it, I simply shrugged O.K. and left.

I didn't call or see Karner again that summer, but one night, weeks later, he called me, upset because of a possible breach of etiquette with the girl next door. They were dating, a surprise to me, who wasn't even thinking about dating. We had never talked about girls. He and Chrissie had come back from a movie and were visiting on the porch swing.

"I had to pee really bad," he said, "and it got worse and worse, till I thought I couldn't hold it any more. I was too embarrassed to ask to use the bathroom, so I made an excuse to go into the backyard by myself and I peed in her mother's petunias. I don't think she saw me. I hope she doesn't think I'm weird. Do you think it was okay?"

All these memories and more came flooding back in an instant as I listened to him now in my mother's living room – all carried on the sound of that voice. It was mellow and musical; its quiet, clever cadences seemed to set the tone and rhythms of the room, as if the whole family had been jolted out of its customary arrangements and reconfigured around this newcomer. Just to belong, I laughed with the others, even though his low, throwaway lines eluded my poor hearing. Twice I broke in, made some studied, clever remark of my own, probably in a voice too strident, a manner too deliberate, only to be met with silence from Karner. A laugh would have been some measure of acknowledgment. Mary laughed; she thinks I'm funny.

Eventually, I couldn't keep up, couldn't track the quick give-and-take, and did what I always do in such situations. I checked out. I listened to the conversation as if through a glass pane. It had no meaning, it was simply an abstract arrangement of sounds, a series of random bursts and rumblings, tinklings and basses, long flowing phrases alternating with short, staccato reports. And through it all, running like a thread through the maze of memory, was the beguiling obbligato of that voice.

What was the source of my anger? This all-too-familiar feeling of isolation in social settings, that went all the way back to childhood? The snub of forty years ago, or the snub here and now? Or did my reaction speak to a greater hurt, some loss too deep for words?

Boys I Never Knew

The grief of the unlived life – we all deal with it in one form or another. For me as a married gay man who came out later in life, however, it has a special poignancy, an existential edge. In some sense, it defines me. That grief lay at the heart of my reaction to Karner. The boy came back to me in all his beauty because that was the only way I could experience him... in retrospect.

I moved through adolescence numb. I shut down my tender and sexual feelings because everything in my culture, spoken and unspoken, told me they were unthinkable, unforgivable. To survive that tumultuous passage into adulthood, I learned to compartmentalize, to exist on two tracks simultaneously, knowing full well who I was with one part of my being, while with the other, more dominant part, fighting and denying it with everything I had. Knowing and denying were like breathing in and breathing out.

I can retrace my adolescence as a series of lost moments. I remember the time in ninth grade when my best buddy, Arizona, said as we were lying on his bed, looking out the window and ogling two girls across the street who were enjoying the unaccustomed warmth of an early spring day: "You know, two boys could have a lot of fun too."

Arizona was a superb athlete, a handsome boy with jet-black hair, a hint of Native American in his features, one of those natural heroes with an easy grace who drew almost everyone to him. I looked at him, lying just two feet away from me, with total incomprehension. What did those words mean? To whom was he saying them? I checked out, the words didn't register. Not then, they didn't, but I have thought of them often since.

And I am left wondering, was it then that I stopped going over to his house almost every day after school? That was our routine. The thought only occurs to me forty-five years later. Arizona and I were very close. The walls of his room were plastered with dozens of zany cartoons in the style of Mad Magazine that I had drawn just for him; he was the friend to whom I had confided my fears that I was jerking off too much. But at some point – I don't know when or why – I simply stopped seeing him. It's one of those curious gaps in my history.

Another occurred with a friend in eleventh grade. I was walking home from downtown Robbinsdale with Denny Nelson, who was going on and on about this girl he was seeing, how wonderful she was and how great it made him feel to have a steady girl.

"I hope you get a girl-friend, Bob. There's nothing like it, nothing like the love of a girl. It makes you feel good about yourself, that you're a man and you care about each other more than anything else in the world."

By this time, almost all the boys I hung out with were talking about girls. I had no interest. One girl was trying to date me, but this only made me vaguely uncomfortable, like something was expected of me. What? – I hadn't a clue. I had an almost determined innocence on the subject. But I liked it when boys talked about girls, even if I felt a little left out. It meant I was accepted, at least as an adjunct member, into the sacred fraternity of boys. I belonged. And it made me feel close to them because they opened up, made themselves vulnerable, in ways not typical between boys.

Denny was usually shy and quiet, but not this afternoon. When we got back to my house, we went into my brother's and my bedroom, closed the door and continued our conversation. He stretched out his lanky frame on my brother's lower bunk, which was U.S. Army surplus and sagged under his weight like a hammock. He clasped his hands behind his head and turned his face toward me to speak. That's the last memory I have of the experience.

I like to imagine his long, thin face, with its well-defined contours, its ridges of brow and cheekbone, the crooked bridge of his nose broken in a fight, looking sensitive and softened in the muted light of late afternoon. What other words we said to each other, what I felt and what I thought afterwards, I don't recall. But the record is clear: I stopped seeing him after that, except for occasional pleasantries at school.

Why? Did I feel stirrings of a forbidden tenderness... attraction, desire? Everything else about the experience is vivid and etched into memory: the walk home, the conversation about girl-friends – it occurred as we crossed the railroad tracks and passed Triangle Park – the scene of Denny lying on the bed, the quality of light in the room. Then memory stops, because feeling stops. The sense of closeness, comforting during the walk home, becomes threatening. I do what I need to do to protect myself without even knowing what I am protecting myself against. I disconnect. I terminate the friendship. The only recollection of feeling I have from that conversation in the bedroom lingers like the remnant of a forgotten dream – something intense and vague that nags at the edge of consciousness and disturbs the day's composure.

But it preserved the memory. Both of these experiences – with Arizona and Denny – while lost to me in certain respects, remain locked into memory, charged with a powerful yet indecipherable emotion. The key to unlocking the fullness of those moments, making sense of my history and recovering the boy I never had a chance to be, I receive only in adulthood, when I am ready to come out and accept myself as a gay man.

How many friendships with boys, and then later with men, followed this pattern of unaccountable termination? How many were short-circuited from ever developing in the first place?

A string of boys passed through my teenage years, appearing mostly in cameo roles, in brief, chance encounters that were much safer to manage than full friendships, and whose main purpose was to feed a starved imagination.

I remember Jerry, a cute, slight, blond go-fer at a resort on Lake Vermillion where my family vacationed the summer after ninth grade. I couldn't wait to finish breakfast every morning so I could hang out with him in the garage as he tinkered with boat motors and told funny stories about resort residents. I visited every chance I got during the day, and always felt a sinking feeling when I didn't find him there, bent over his workbench. I was jealous of his attentions to the other residents, and felt uneasy when he invited me to go riding with him and his buddies as they picked up girls in the nearby town of Tower. All I wanted was to be near him.

One morning he told me, with a sly wink and grin, about Jimmy, who had stuck his finger up a girl, then passed it around for the other guys in the car to smell. "Boy, did it stink!," he said, chuckling. I thought this was crude and disrespectful to the girl, and wondered why she would let anyone do this to her.

Jerry seemed the master of everything he touched: motors, broken fishing reels, the pike and pan fish he gutted and scaled for the residents, and I suppose, even girls. I was in seventh heaven when he wanted to learn something I knew – how to do Art Deco lettering, something I had learned from an old sign-painting book my grandpa had given to me.

In that intense, too-short week, Jerry-charmed, I learned everything I could about him, his habits, thoughts, history, likes and dislikes. His life was mythical, every fact of it enchanted. I learned he liked quick-draw target shooting and that became the most fascinating topic in the world. Before my family left for home, I asked my dad to take me into Tower to a gun shop where I could buy Jerry a quick-draw holster. I included a note with the extravagant gift, which I laid reverentially at the shrine of his unattended workbench the morning we left, inviting him to visit me sometime in Robbinsdale. For at least two summers after that, I wondered if he would showup.

All of these activities – the fascination and obsession, the disappointment and jealousy, the gift and longing – grew bit by bit, a great sacred edifice encrusted around a mysterious, hollow core of something I couldn't name or acknowledge. I was an acolyte performing the meaningless rituals of a forgotten religion.

Two years after Jerry came Jack, the son of one of my dad's best friends, who paid a brief visit with his father one grey fall afternoon on a day-trip down from Duluth. We played catch with a football in the leaf-swept street in front of my house, running crazily after passes and punts skewed by the skittish wind. We ended the game hot and sweaty, exhausted and laughing. Jack suggested a quick shower together. Together? He was husky, ruddy and affable, more developed than I was and obviously more comfortable being naked in the company of other boys. I barely looked at him as we undressed in the tiny bathroom and stepped into the shower, and I kept my back to him, careful not to brush against him in the cramped quarters. By this time, I was skilled at self-containment – lots of practice turning to the wall and hunching over to undress in boy's locker-rooms, studiously averting my eyes and shutting out the sounds of laughter.

For years after Jack's visit, however, I was much less reserved in fantasy, though never reckless. I revisited the scene again and again to bask in boyish affection. I had my fill of his frank good looks, his playful good nature; without shame I watched him undress, soap himself up and towel off in the safety zone of my imagination. No sex. These fantasies, countless scenarios salvaged from my few scraps of memory – whatever I had allowed myself to experience at the time – were about something unnamable, vague and idealized, and always tinged with yearning and regret. What had I missed?

My teenage years were dotted with such encounters, though they grew fewer as I grew older. I lived increasingly on the memory of a select few, which sustained me through an increasingly lonely adolescence.

Chief among these encounters – the most powerful, the one I returned to most often – was the boy I met one summer when I was sixteen on a family camping trip to Lake Itasca. I came upon him sitting by himself on a grassy knoll in a clearing at the edge of the lake. I can't retrieve the actual memory any more. It is too embellished and shop-worn, shrouded in layers of association. All that remains is a picture, a feeling. He is hunched forward, his elbows resting cavalierly on his knees, gazing across the water, his profile stark against its shimmering surface and cocked attentively to the far shore, a long stem of grass pinched between his lips. In silhouette, he is reduced to a few clean strokes, all angles, poised, the grace of energy in repose. I meet him as I break out of the brush after straying off the path through the woods. Did the suddenness of the encounter disarm us, create an instant rapport? Camaraderie – that's the core feeling. We had a brief conversation, that was all. I quickly forgot the content, the particulars. They weren't important. What mattered was memory. He became a cipher. With no name, no history, no face, he stood for any boy with whom I could feel close, and therefore, no boy. He was a screen onto which I could project anything I wanted, a trigger that released a flood of emotion. In countless returns to the scene, each one elaborated with minute variations, I drew whatever comfort I could from the core feelings of openness and closeness, which were magnified in imagination into a dream of impossible tenderness. Did we go for a swim, a walk in the woods, did we talk about our boyhood, our dreams and plans for the future? In conversation after conversation, that dream of closeness was refracted again and again, held up to the light of a wholly imaginary life. The incident became hallowed, part of the lore of my growing up. It sustained me through my later adolescence and the early years of my marriage.

Thin gruel, I think now. And underneath nagged darker feelings: an impossible perfectionism, a bitter disappointment with life and a sense of personal failure and cowardice. I could not seize the moment. Could I even love? But what would I seize, and what would I love? And what really happened in that clearing? Anything? All this fretting and yearning and grieving were about something that never happened, never could happen, because I would not admit to myself what was going on.

By the time of my late teens, therefore, I was profoundly lonely – "bone-lonely," I used to call it. Because I had no interest in girls, and because boys were strictly off-limits, I felt paralyzed, and I saw this paralysis as an inability to love, a deep moral flaw at the core of my being that set me apart from the rest of humanity.

Gary at Poolside

You're a bolt of pink neon, jagged in tremulous blue. You dive deep with scissored kicks, skim the gritty bottom of the pool with your pug nose, shimmy along its Jello geometry, then twist and roll in rapid ascent. You shatter the shimmering film between us, leaving a pearly cream of bubbles in your wake. Dazzling efflorescence! You arch your back, loll lazily on the rippling surface and bare your smooth belly to my gaze. Your navel glistens, a tufted path points to jewels bobbing in the cleft of your groin.

None of this I saw then, not as I watched guardedly from pool's edge, watched the watcher watching. A studied scene: two boys swimming naked at the Y. I was relieved we were the only ones, relieved I watched without desire. It was like looking at snapshots taken with my Brownie Hawkeye: Gary at poolside, Gary poised on diving board, Gary blurred in mid-air and holding his nose while doing the cannonball. Each shot separate, contained, composed, in muted shades of grey and slightly out of focus, and every one taken from too far away.

But months later I watched again, this time in

sweet, shameful secrecy, watched as my family drove through the Badlands of South Dakota. I studied those shots again and again, up close and from every angle, tried to charge them with the vivid life I'd missed before. Not quite you, Gary, none of that boyish exuberance poised just this side of manly grace, none of that holy fire. But enough, enough to stir me as I sat hot and cramped between my younger brother and maiden Aunt Augusta in the back seat of our '53 Studebaker.

Now, I watch again, reclaim in imagining what was nearly lost to memory. Shame streams from me like bubbles from a swimmer breaking for the surface, and you flash before me, more vivid and electric with each bold stroke.

At the time we went swimming, Gary was legendary in the neighborhood. He was rumored to be big – boys kept careful track of these things. The subject came up over Pepsis and baseball cards as I sat outside the corner grocery store with the Swanson kids and their new friend Franko, a tall, thin kid who wore sweatshirts even on the hottest summer days to hide his skinny arms.

"Gary's huge," one of them said.

"Bigger than Oberg?"

"You bet."

"You gotta be kidding. How do you know? You seen it?"

"Naw, but everybody who's seen it says so."

"Nobody's bigger than Oberg."

Let them talk, I thought, I'll soon see for myself. Gary had pestered me for months to go swimming at the downtown YMCA where, in those days, men and boys swam in the nude. I was reluctant – I was as skinny as

Franko and slow to develop – but I had finally relented, and we were set to go. When the day arrived and I had steeled myself for the ordeal, it was as if secret emissaries from the Vatican had been dispatched to sanitize the scene. The offending genitalia had, in effect, been air-brushed out. Call it a supreme act of will, a triumph of my eternal vigilance. I saw nothing, or I remembered nothing, or what I saw was so nondescript, so eviscerated of life, it counted for nothing.

What I learned as a defense mechanism in adolescence – turning myself off to a present experience and recovering it later, at a safe remove, where its potency was diluted with longing and disappointment, and I could manage it within the strictures of conscious intention – became a reflex, an escape in early adulthood. Now, in the fullness of middle age, retrospection has become a means of healing. In coming out, I reclaim myself and my history. In remembering the boy Gary or the boy Karner or any of the boys who passed through my adolescence, I remember the boy Robert, and in paying attention to unaccountable gaps in my history, to my anger, bitterness or any emotion that takes its charge from deeper wellsprings, I honor the loss and self-betrayal that boy endured… and I move beyond them.

Remembering is a holy and healing act. For me the word means precisely that: a "re-membering," a piecing together of a fractured life, making it whole. *whole, holy, healing; Remembering, re-membering* – words have curious associations. In reference to Gary, "re-membering" acquires another dimension entirely.

In coming out, with that act of radical self-acceptance, I begin to make sense of my story, and a curious synergy happens: the more integrated and actualized I become, the more freely memory flows for me, as if lending a hand in the process. This is active, shaping memory, not chance recollection or idle reminiscence. It is memory telling me what my life is about, where I have been and where I am going. It sifts and reorganizes, directs my attention, fills in the gaps and makes vital connections. It is revelatory, dynamic and organic, an energy that breathes through the raw materials of my life, showing me its pattern, telling me its story. The boundaries between remembering and imagining, between child and adult, between past, present and future, between actual and potential, are blurred, as my story unfolds, takes shape in the telling.

Where to begin?

SURVIVAL

The Dream

I'm walking down a dusty country road that winds through sunlit fields and gloomy woods. The road dips, bend, forks and disappears into the distance. I feel lost and scared, uncertain of the way, but I am determined, drawn by my mission, to rescue and heal my Uncle Harry who lies sick and dying in a land far away. Then I find myself in a close, shuttered room standing at his bedside, gazing into his pale, pea-green face. I feel sickly sweet inside, like I am melting.

As nearly as I can tell, I first had this dream when I was three or four years old. It dates from a time before conscious memory but I recall lying awake at night until I was eight or nine years old, watching the moonlight throw spooky shadows on the walls while trying to re-cover this dream from long ago. I had a trick – "taking pinchers," I called it. I'd grab the corrugated edge of the sheet with one hand, stretch it taut to get just the right tension and rub it back and forth underneath the finger-nails of my other hand until my tongue flattened against the roof of my mouth and I slipped into a trance. There, if I was lucky, I could re-enter that magical dream.

Most of the details of the original dream have long since been lost to me, but ritual and memory have preserved intact its core: the basic plot, my intense feelings and, remarkably, the peculiar color of my uncle's face. What I know from the historical record is this: at the time of the original dream my father was away serving in the army, possibly already stationed on Guam, and my mother says I was feeling abandoned; my uncle, a navy airman, had been shot down and rescued in the southern Pacific. A blond, blue-eyed Finlander, the latter looks stunningly handsome in uniform in his wedding photograph – I had good taste in men even then!

Was it that ridiculous color that made me eventually abandon the dream?. For years I could work this spell, enter its charmed circle almost at will, calling down upon myself all its tender sweetness and healing power, but with repeated use it lost its potency and began to seem merely childish and silly. I held onto it as long as I could, but gradually, reluctantly, relinquished it, all the while grieving its passing. The fact remained, however, that dream and its spell, and the long shadow it cast over my childhood, made me different, and somehow I knew that difference had to be kept hidden. That was part of the charm.

Different. I knew I was different from almost before memory. I didn't have a word for it then, not even "different." It was a sense more than anything else, a sense of being marked, set apart. Dreams, memory, reverie, slipping in and out of ordinary reality – the sense of difference went that deep.

In all the years that followed, even in the midst of my deepest denial, the frayed and faded remnants of that dream remained with me, a reminder, calling me home.

The Authorized Version

I used to like to tell a story. This was years ago, before I came out as a gay man. The wise adult was speaking, telling a cheery tale about how I learned to run and throw like a boy. it went something like this...

One day after school, while running in the fields near Blueberry Hill, Robert and his friends were joined by a stranger to the neighborhood, a new boy at school, who quickly took the lead in their games. Robert had noticed him in the halls, one of those natural heroes starting to surface in sixth grade, handsome, poised and already well-formed. He took Robert aside and said, gently, without reproach, "You're running and throwing like a girl. Look, this is how a boy runs." And he dug his right foot into the ground, kicking up a spray of dirt as he sped away, leaning his whole body into his long, loping stride, his arms pumping at his sides, his hands grabbing at the air for extra traction. He circled back and stopped, breathless. "O.K., now you do it." And Robert copied what he saw, running round the boy, who coached him on.

"O.K." Then the boy picked up a smooth, flat rock and handed it to Robert saying, "This is how a boy throws." He took Robert's arm and brought it all the way back behind his head and out to the side in a wide arc, where Robert held the stone steady between his thumb and forefinger. "Now watch," And the boy picked up another rock and pitched it forward, stepping into the throw with his left leg and following through with his whole upper body, and the stone sailed free, high across the field. "Now you do it, it's real easy." Robert copied what he saw until he got it right. He was a good pupil.

It was so simple once it was pointed out. Of course, boys and girls ran and threw differently; they did almost everything differently. Why hadn't he figured this out for himself if he was so smart? Robert liked this boy. Who wouldn't take instruction from such a wise and gentle teacher? From that day forth, Robert noticed, he did things differently, and life was lots easier.

As an adult I told this story many times, in many ways, poking gentle fun at myself. This was the authorized version of my growing up. Being able to tell my story with amused detachment, laughing over dinner or drinks, provided a measure of comfort and release in an otherwise tightly controlled existence. It allowed me to disclose certain facts about myself, while masking others.

Denial is a funny thing. The story is, in all its particulars, true; even the tone is true. I felt the generosity of the boy's gesture, the comfort of being received into the sacred fraternity of boys. But something can be true, and not true at the same time. There is, in the bland optimism of the tale, a brutal denial of the reality of that boy's life.

Herewith, the unvarnished version of how I learned to run and throw like a boy, though I suspect that some day I will begin this story too with the tag, "I used to like to tell a story..."

Bullies and Sissies

Roberta, Roberta... Sometimes, when I'm doing my calisthenics at the gym, I think people are watching me. I know it's nuts, but I start to sweat, my timing and breathing go to hell, and suddenly I'm flopping around like a demented rag-doll. I've slipped into one of those dark places from childhood. I can almost hear the bitter taunt from years ago, the click of those heels behind me... *Roberta, Roberta.*

I've always hated the name "Robert." I used to say, it was the formality of the name, the wall it set between me and others; "Bob," the nickname of adolescence and adulthood, meant acceptance and fitting in. Anyway, that was the authorized version. Truth is, however, I hated the name "Robert" because it rubbed my nose in my childhood. Now you could say my childhood was no worse than most; it sure wasn't as bad as Tom Breen's, or some other boys I could name. But I was a sensitive kid, and as I like to say in my more philosophical moments, everybody and everything suffers perfectly, according to their nature.

The awful thing about the name "Robert" was that

it took just one letter, one lousy letter, and you'd slipped over the line – it became a girl's name. That line was terribly important growing up, and for me, it was very tricky walking it.

I could say, I was a sissy, but it went deeper than that. Yeah, I ran and threw like a girl; I liked hanging around my mom and her friends when they came over for coffee; and I liked staying home from school to watch her favorite TV shows, like "The Big Payoff" and "Queen for a Day." Sometimes at school during recess I hid in the cloakroom so I could stay indoors to draw and paint while the other kids went outside to play dodge ball or kickball.

Now don't get me wrong, I wasn't any mamma's boy. I could scrap with the best of them, like the time I wrestled Ronnie Margolis and pinned his shoulders to the sidewalk when he kept calling me "*Yal-da, yal-da*, boy-girl, boy-girl!" He had found a use for his newly learned Hebrew, and I didn't like it one bit. I could call on a boy-kind of fierceness when I had to, but I wore my boyhood uneasily, like an acquired taste.

No, it went deeper than the way I giggled and laughed and carried my books. Maybe it was the funny way I sometimes felt about men, but I suspect it went deeper still. It went as deep as the dream.

Roberta, Roberta… Jakes had a way of saying that word, drawing it out and shifting the inflection from syllable to syllable, investing each new pronunciation with an insinuating lilt more poisonous than the last. That word, on his lips, said everything.

I was new to seventh grade, just getting my footing in the strange new school. Jakes was a hood, a whole new class of bullies to contend with. He wore his long hair in a ducktail, his shirt collar turned up, his pants low on his hips, his belt-buckle turned to the side. He strutted and swaggered, rolling his shoulders and swinging his arms loosely at his sides as he walked, his hands cupped in half-fists. As if striking sparks, his cleated black boots clicked out a menacing rhythm on the slick schoolhouse floors.

I knew all about bullies. Lee Elementary had been full of them. But I had learned to take precautions; I had memorized all the safe routes to and from school. By sixth grade, the pieces of a grand strategy had fallen into place: stay quiet and out of trouble, stick to the sidelines, and above all, don't shine, don't shine. Notice was fatal to boys like me. By sixth grade, I was relieved to discover I had joined the ranks of the kids who all through grade school had seemed to stand a head taller than the rest. I walked to school more confident and secure, with a smaller knot in the pit of my stomach.

Then came the shift to Regent High. We sixth-graders were snot-nosed kids again. Jakes must have spotted me right away – a weak gazelle on the fringe of the herd – and he smelled blood. Some 2,000 kids were packed into the ancient, sprawling three-story structure; at the sound of the bell, we all scrambled to get to the next class on time. Gone was the security of one room, one teacher, one set of standards; in its place was a whole new pecking-order, still to be determined, and a maze of rules and expectations as bewildering as the long dim corridors and twisting staircases that branched into warrens of classrooms and offices. On the first day of school, the smell of sweeping compound, pungent with its heady mix of excitement and anxiety, almost made me retch.

Jakes had a sidekick, and together they made an odd pair. While Jakes had the build and sullen good looks of a boy two or three years older and was feared and admired by the other boys, Larry was unremarkable except for his alliance with Jakes. Short and scrawny, with a beakish nose and bobbing Adam's apple, he jerked his head when he talked and peered at you with wide, blank blue eyes through round spectacles. The crooked plates of his skull shone through the dull sheen of his close-cropped heinie.

Did I smell danger? I tried once or twice, before the persecution began, to get on Jakes' good side. More likely, my overtures were part of a general campaign of appeasement begun at the start of each new school year. When Mrs. Mulcahy, the social studies teacher, assigned me to sit with Jakes during a classroom exercise, I relied on my usual tactic of ingratiating myself. I helped him with the questions; I flattered and encouraged him. He didn't look at me, and only slouched further down in his seat. His wavy dark-brown hair hung low on his forehead and curled behind his ears and down into his collar; his eyes, with their dreamy lids and long, curly lashes, were crusty with sleep. In response to my pleasantries, he grunted and shifted his weight ominously, occasionally sneering a reply, totally unmoved by the charm that worked so well with adults. Frankly, it wasn't working all that well with them any more. When I presented my oral report on the Ku Klux Klan, cobbled from the scant paragraphs in the 1903 encyclopedia moldering in our basement, Mrs. Mulcahy reproved me in front of the class:

"Mr. Anderson, you need to check several sources before giving a report, for accuracy and completeness. Your source is obviously dated and biased in favor of an organization with a long history of suppressing the civil rights of Negroes." It wasn't fair; she didn't criticize Jakes when he talked about customizing street-rods, which as far as I could tell, had nothing to do with social studies.

How were you supposed to know how to behave, and how could you possibly please so many different teachers at once? At Lee Elementary, my report card had glittered with gold and silver stars; I had been passed from spinster teacher to spinster teacher like a prize – "You'll like this one," Miss Rolfe, my second-grade teacher, had told Miss Nelson, soon to be my third-grade teacher. I even went back for lap visits. That was until I discovered it was dangerous to shine too much; by sixth grade I managed to get myself into just enough trouble.

I had it all figured out, I thought. Not to figure it out was fatal. You were always being watched and pushed and tested, by teachers and classmates alike, in school and out, to see how you fit in, measured up or fell short; and for boys, the process was often brutal. Every grade had its pariah; in fifth grade, it was Leonard Elfman, in sixth, Thom Munson. Tom Breen held the dubious distinction of being the all-school pariah. He was a mixed-race kid in a white-bread suburban school in the unenlightened Fifties, and no self-respecting boy, including me, ever peed in Breen's urinal. A slight, quiet boy with a dark tan complexion, shy brown eyes and full lips, he had a shock of coarse black hair that angled like a hatchet across his forehead. The butt of jokes and taunts, he was the kid everybody talked about behind his back. "Nigger," "half-breed," "faggot," "moron" – any epithet would do; he was the one kid nobody wanted to be like. To be Not-Breen was to possess at least a scrap of status in the cut-throat world of childhood. In all his years at

Lee, I don't remember Breen having one friend. I didn't want to end up like Breen, nobody did.

Roberta, Roberta... The taunts began shortly after the episode in Mrs. Mulcahy's class. I was rushing to get to English class on time when I heard the name behind me, followed by the click of those heels.

"Hey, sissy! Little momma's boy, where'ya goin' with your books high up there like a girl. What'ya hidin'?" I blushed. I had neglected a basic rule. My hand and wrist were tired from carrying my books at my side, against my hip, where they were slipping out of my grip with every step I took. For just a moment, I was cradling them in my arm against my chest. The penalty was swift and severe. Jakes gave my shoulder a rough shove that sent my books and papers flying onto the floor, then marched smartly across my English theme, giving it a wicked twist with his heel. Larry sniggered on the sidelines. "Pansy," he hissed as he brushed past.

Divide and conquer was my next strategy. Larry was the weak link, and I would try to get on his good side. He was in my music class, and out of Jakes' shadow, worked hard to shine on his own. I bantered with Larry and the boys during class and was more disruptive than usual, earning two reprimands from Mr. Adams... and I hoped a good word from Larry. I laughed louder than the other boys when Larry farted or told sexual jokes, most of which I barely understood.

My crowning achievement, the worst deed I could muster, occurred one day while Mr. Adams played symphonic pieces on the phonograph to teach us how to identify various composers. I had saved a test tube of pig's blood salvaged from my mother's pork roast from the previous Sunday. I tested it each day, waiting till it smelled really rank, then brought my treasure to class where I let Larry use it to torment the girls. He and the other boys passed it back and forth in front of the girls, shoving it under their noses and threatening to pour it on their dresses. Their muffled shrieks and the cackling of the boys got lost in the cannon shots and thundering climax of the *1812 Overture*. I reveled in the excitement and vicarious wickedness, but without a follow-up act, my notoriety was short-lived.

In the hallways, the names and shoving continued. *Roberta, Roberta...* I'd hear the mocking strains from somewhere out of the crowd of students thronging the halls. I varied my route, even risked being late for class, but I never knew where they'd strike next. I'd be walking down the hall minding my own business when I'd hear this loud whispering and laughing behind me, and the inevitable approach of those heels... slap, slap, SLAP!

"Did you drop this?," Jakes shrieked as he waved a girl's handkerchief high in the air before stuffing it down the front of my shirt. Then he yanked out my shirttails, gave me a kick and Larry tried to trip me.

This couldn't be happening to me. I had escaped notice all through grade school. I was so careful, in every detail, including avoiding the wrong sort of associations. I had rebuffed overtures from Leonard Elfman, the squat, bullet-headed, pasty-faced pariah of fifth grade. I got stuck going to his house one afternoon, and was relieved once the invitations stopped and I no longer had to cook up phony excuses. None too soon either – that spring a gang of boys pushed him into an ice bank, and he ran home crying with bloody palms. I saw him from time to time after that, walking home by himself on the other side of the street, and I felt embarrassed for him. It was best to avoid packs of kids – the easiest way to stay out of trouble. Besides, with my poor hearing, I couldn't follow the funny give-and-take of their banter; I either had to fake responses or risk not hearing something addressed to me, or worse yet, replying when it wasn't. Alone was good – and better to be embarrassed for Elfman than for myself.

Thom Munson was the kid who sought me out in sixth grade. He was a thin asthmatic boy with dark-rimmed glasses, owlish eyes and a soft, reedy voice. Not a pariah exactly, but probably somebody else to avoid. Who spells "Tom" with an "h" anyway? He'd find me during recess and together we'd haunt the fringes of the playground, seeking refuge behind hills or clumps of trees to avoid conscription into the remorseless games. We were always the last to be picked for softball, the first eliminated in dodge ball. Once, as we walked along the nearby railroad tracks kicking up loose gravel, he found a shiny Liberty half-dollar that he shared with me at the corner store after school. He invited me over for dinner one Sunday evening to hear a favorite recording of his, by the Vienna Boy's Choir. As we listened to the scratchy 78 in his father's book-lined study, he leaned over and whispered to me, "They used to castrate boys to keep their voices high and pure like this." The way he said it gave me the creeps. Definitely somebody else to avoid – I had a nose for these things.

This tactic had worked so well in grade school. I was using it right now to keep my distance from Roy Colver, a tall, sensitive-looking kid with blond hair who had invited me over one Saturday morning to see his stamp and coin collections. He was bright and well-spoken, and during lunch hour sat gossiping and giggling with the girls. The boys were whispering behind his back. Months after my visit, I saw him standing on a street corner talking and laughing with some girls while I rode by on the bus. I watched him toss his head and smile, his hands fluttering near his mouth like birds, and felt grateful I had escaped entanglement. Why did I always attract these characters anyway? – they were nothing but trouble. In any case, after only a few weeks of seventh grade, nothing was working any more; my grand strategy was unraveling.

It wasn't fair. I had given up so much. The hardest thing was shining – I liked to shine. I could forgo the gold and silver stars, the samples of my Palmer penmanship hanging in the hallway display cases at Lee. But it wasn't till fifth-grade that I gave up performing skits in secret behind the schoolhouse garage for small claques of kids who hooted and howled as I did bits from the latest Uncle Miltie or Lucy shows, parodies of Camille expiring on her deathbed, and bitchy phone conversations by Tallulah Bankhead.

By sixth grade, that boy had gone underground, to surface only occasionally in the presumed security of his neighborhood – as flamboyant impresario of basement carnivals or summer sidewalk parades, or in games of pretend played with his younger brother's friends, boys four years his junior. There, for a time, he still felt safe.

The harassment continued. My only refuge was my classes. There, under the jurisdiction of adults, I felt secure, even though their rules were more exacting than in grade school, their manner and expectations more impersonal, less comforting. But outside the classroom, I felt vulnerable. Between classes, during free time or lunch hour, and especially in boy's gym, where rough-housing and bullying were the norm, I was completely at the mercy of Jakes and Larry. I skipped gym as often as I could, relying on an old tactic of going to the nurse's office with an upset stomach. The knot was back, bigger than ever, but the nurse at Regent was less sympathetic than the nurse at Lee, and usually sent me back to class after a brief rest.

I had never liked gym, and I liked it even less now that I was being told, by other boys, not just Jakes and Larry, that I looked like a girl running from player to player on the basketball court – it was always the Skins against the Shirts – sliding crazily in my stockinged feet on the slick wood floors, wildly flailing my arms in front of the faces of the other players to block their shots. I had been proud of my performance; I thought I was doing exactly what was expected of me. But there was something missing, something fundamental I wasn't picking up – some way of moving, an attitude, an energy, a whole way of being that was alien to me. It was something more than a discrete, learnable set of skills. What was it?

It was as if suddenly the whole world was in code, and I hadn't been given the key. What I did know was that to be called a sissy, to be compared to a girl, was just about the worst thing that could happen to a boy. Somehow, by a curious twist in the rules, a mysterious change in the environment, every gesture had become sexually charged. It went beyond how you carried your books and ran and threw and talked and giggled and played basketball and liked hanging around your mother's friends. Behavior that was perfectly innocent in a child was now singled out for ridicule and rebuke. The correction might be cruelly or kindly administered; often, it was imparted in hushed tones, with a sense of profound embarrassment on both sides.

Not by Jakes and Larry, however. They were merciless. They took to marching silently beside me in the halls, mimicking my every move. I tried to ignore them and the looks of my fellow classmates; I reverted to a technique I had used whenever danger threatened in grade school – I checked out, I pretended it wasn't happening to me.

They began spitting on me, on my shirt and face. Larry came into his own here. He coughed up a thick wad of phlegm, formed this wicked tube with his tongue, then fired with deadly aim and force. Splat! He got me right between the eyes, where the gob stuck for a second before sliding slowly down the bridge of my nose, where it hung precariously from the tip. Larry sniggered, and I heard the sound of those cleated boots fade into the distance. I walked straight ahead, not varying my pace, looking neither left nor right. I didn't see my classmates, and they didn't see me. I was invisible. I didn't wipe the spit off till I was safely seated in class. There, I re-engaged. At night, at home, I put it all away. It wasn't happening to me. It had happened to those poor unfortunates at Lee – Elfman, Munson, Breen. It was happening right now to broad-hipped, moon-faced Max, a boy who shared my workbench in wood shop. He muttered and fussed over his projects, scurrying from bench to bench and pestering the other boys with his silly questions and comments. Didn't he know he was supposed to keep quiet? One day he had leaned across the project clamped in his vise, a ramshackle birdhouse with uneven corners, and whispered to me conspiratorially: "Do you know what I read yesterday? – that Tchaikovsky was a HOMO-sexual!"

What the hell did I care what Tchaikovsky was, and what the hell was a HOMO-sexual anyway? I wished people would just leave me alone. Maybe it was happening to Max, but it wasn't happening to me.

Eventually, Jakes and Larry got bored, or found another victim. Eventually, I figured things out and made what could be called, in the parlance of the times, a more-or-less successful adjustment. I noticed, I did things differently, and life was lots easier. It didn't come without a struggle, however. It took hours of anguished praying in the restless pre-dawn darkness that God, in his infinite mercy, would make me other than I was. It took months of saying over and over to myself as I walked to school every morning, like a sacred mantra: "Boys are hard, bad; girls are soft, good; boys are hard, bad; girls are soft, good." Tricks, maybe, but consciousness is a funny thing.

By ninth grade, on a dare from my buddy Arizona, I could practically think myself into having an erection while walking past Janet Annakala's desk. She was the best stacked girl in class. Arizona even wrote a poem to commemorate the occasion:

> *Spring has sprung,*
> *Robert has also.*
> *The thing that sprung*
> *Is between his balls-o.*

So what if my boner, in some sense, was bogus; so, it was rumored, were Janet's tits.

Eventually I dated, and eventually I married. By then I could think myself into practically anything.

Now, my story may be a little melodramatic. I

didn't get my brains bashed out in a urinal like that un-fortunate sailor who made a pass at a straight man in the bathroom of a San Diego bar; I wasn't crucified on a lonely country fence like that college student in Wyo-ming; I wasn't driven to suicide like the high school kid in Wisconsin. I wasn't Tom Breen. But I was a sensitive kid, and as I like to say in my more philosophical moments, everybody and everything suffers perfectly, according to their nature.

Elegy

Roberta, Roberta... You descend the basement stairs, putting on with each step more and more of its darkness and mystery. Your heart pounds with excitement as you skip lightly down the last few steps. In these moments, the place of night terrors becomes a passage to that fairy world that is fast slipping away from you. You pass through the root cellar, with its jars of pickles and preserves gleaming in the scant rays filtering through the cobwebs in the high narrow window, and enter the dim slanted chamber under the stairs. From the steel trunk tucked in its narrowest angle you take the musty red-plaid ruffled curtains, unfold and shake them out, and remove your t-shirt. The cool damp envelopes you. You wind one of the drapes tightly around your waist, the other around your torso, leaving one shoulder bare. You clasp your mother's rhinestone necklace around your forehead, fix the winged pendant just above the bridge of your nose, and step out into the mote-filled light of the root cellar. Twirling, twirling, you fling your arms up and out, letting the flounce fly free from your body, scattering the dust motes into the shadows.

You are Princess Azura, and when you rejoin your brother's friends waiting in the back yard, each with his assigned role – Leslie, the strongest and handsomest, is Flash Gordon – the play begins. Imperious, stung by his repeated rebuke, your amber pendant flashing like an evil third eye, you banish the hapless space cadet to the fiery dungeons of your father, Ming the Merciless.

"Torture him, torture him!," you cry, directing your minions to their stations.

Was it a cutting remark, too many sniggers, or David Hawes taking you aside one afternoon to share, in confidence, what his father had told him the night before? As you both inched along the pitched top of the retaining wall, keeping your footing by grabbing the fence pickets hand over hand, he said in hushed tones, so the other boys wouldn't hear:

"My dad told me and my brother at dinner last night that you're different, not like other boys, and we're supposed to treat you special, with respect." What did it mean – "different, special" – and why did it hurt, why did it feel both good and bad to be treated with such kindness? You were only being yourself. What did they know that you didn't?

It's hard to say what finally broke through, or when. Consciousness is a funny thing: a person can know something and not know it at the same time. But somewhere in the rough landscape between sixth, seventh and eighth grade, you, the boy who moved through mists of dream and imagination, who was most real and alive in a world of make-believe and intense emotion, disappeared. You yourself were banished.

Oh, Roberta, Roberta...

First Crush

We had man teachers for the first time in seventh grade, and Mr. Hanson, my wood shop teacher, was the cutest one. Cute wasn't even an issue till then, but that was a time of many firsts, including shop, which with my poor hearing I thought was "chop" until one day my dad corrected me with a laugh. It was all new and scary, this shift to a new school, and without knowing it, or more to the point, without knowing what it meant, I had developed a crush on Mr. Hanson.

Rodney was his first name. It was important to know the first names of teachers, even though you could never use them. They were secret, unsayable names, like Yahweh in the Old Testament, and provided an intimate glimpse into the private lives of these mysterious, powerful beings. For me, Rodney became the cutest name in the universe.

Mr. Hanson had wavy brown hair, with a curl that sometimes hung in the middle of his forehead, like Superman. He had clear blue eyes and a deep cleft in his chin. A gap showed between his two front teeth, which gleamed when he smiled. His forearms were strong and furry, and sometimes I could see hair peeping over his white tee-shirt. He didn't have to wear a tie like the other man teachers. He smiled cute, laughed cute, wrapped his big muscular hands around the plane and hammer cute, and when he stood behind me and reached his arms around me to show me something about my poor under-sized project, clamped in the vise in front of us – how the corners weren't square or the sanding was uneven – something within me gave, and I went all soft and mushy inside.

It was all of a piece: the newness and promise of seventh grade, the division of the world into boy and girl things like shop and home ec, tagging along with Joe Miller on chilly fall afternoons as he peddled his papers, and the funny way I sometimes felt around Mr. Hanson. To stand close to him, to receive his practical wisdom, to have conferred upon me the immense gift of his belief in my abilities, was to be given a clue about the mystery of manhood itself, and an insight into the very nature of the universe – how it worked according to certain fixed rules, and how, if you understood and followed those rules, it would yield to your prowess, whatever its apparent chaos and inscrutability. That was the promise of this magical time. It was all of a piece.

A few weeks into fall quarter, I started hanging around school after classes let out. I was curious about this strange new building with its maze of corridors and cubbyholes, and I wanted to know more about Mr. Hanson than his first name. I'd peek down the stairs to see if he was still in the classroom; I didn't dare go down and talk to him, but if I didn't see him, I'd prowl the halls, one floor after another, repeating the pattern, restless till I caught a glimpse of him, in faculty meetings or in casual conversations with other teachers. How I envied them their contact with this man. Then I went home happy.

In the mornings I sometimes walked to school with Mrs. Steffanson, my science teacher, who lived on the next block. She was a kind, pleasant woman, and we talked about school and science and how I planned to be a doctor when I grew up.

"You'll need to know lots of science then," she said.

But I wanted to talk about Mr. Hanson. I asked if she knew him. "I have him for wood shop, and he's a real good teacher." Of course I didn't say he was cute. Mom had corrected me one night when I came out to the kitchen while she was doing the dishes – I had been watching my favorite TV show – and told her I thought the Lone Ranger was cute. I had a crush on him too.

"Men aren't cute, they're handsome," she said. This was useful information, I thought. But in the sharpness of her tone, I took another message: I needed to be careful what I shared about my feelings about men – they were precious, private.

Mrs. Steffanson told me that she liked Mr. Hanson too, and mentioned that his folks came from the same place in Wisconsin as hers. Milwaukee was added to the ever-growing magic circle of information.

I got braver. If I saw Mr. Hanson cleaning up after classes, I hung around the large storage area near the shops, minding my own business, sometimes sitting on the stairs and doing my homework. I'd sit near the edge of the step, leaning forward, looking up from time to time, anxious in case he disappeared without my knowing it. Sometimes he'd say good night as he passed me on the stairs.

Then one day I got my wish. He leaned around the corner, smiled that smile and asked if I wanted to help him clean up.

"Sure," I said, low-key, gathering up my books and jacket. It was important to be cool. School was about more than plotting graphs and diagramming sentences; it was about developing a certain attitude, displaying the right manners and fitting in. He showed me a few simple chores, and I quickly got to work while he reviewed projects and entered grades in his book. I'd show him, I'd make up for my miserable birdhouse. I used the long hooked pole to close the tall wire-mesh windows overlooking the tennis courts, and returned stray tools to the storage area up front. I knew exactly where they went, they fit like pieces in a puzzle. I brushed the sawdust off the large wooden workbenches and swept the concrete floors clean using the wide push broom and plenty of sweet-smelling red sweeping compound.

Some nights we walked home together. It was approaching Halloween – I was wondering if I could still get away with trick-or-treating. I knew some other boys my age who were going out; they weren't even going to wear costumes. It was getting colder and darker outside, and the trees had lost most of their leaves.

I already knew where he lived; early in the school year I had looked up the address in the phone book – I couldn't believe teachers were listed. I knew that the actor who played the Lone Ranger, Clayton Moore – it was hard to believe he was really an actor – owned a home in Golden Valley, right next to Robbinsdale, but you can bet *he* wasn't listed in the phone book! I wondered what he looked like under his mask. The story about Tonto nursing him back to health in a secret cave somewhere in the

Texas hills, protecting him from the gang of desperados who had almost killed him, was another thing that made me feel funny inside. I kept the comic book with that story hidden in the back of a cabinet where nobody could find it. Secrets, feeling funny, private lives, childhood vanishing like the days of summer – it was getting to be an epidemic.

There, in small print, in the perfectly ordinary phone book, was Mr. Hanson's name and address. Rodney. He lived only three blocks from me; we were practically neighbors. I had taken to tagging along with Joe Miller just before dinnertime, as he peddled the evening paper. He was a clean-cut kid, easy and confident, and even though he mostly ignored me, I liked just hanging around him, as if some of what was so likable about him might rub off on me. But mainly I hoped to catch sight of Mr. Hanson, who lived on Joe's route. Maybe I'd see him raking the yard or bringing home groceries; maybe he'd see me with Joe and I'd say "Hi," cool-like.

Yet this was better – here I was, walking home with him. I could see his breath in the crisp air, feel his warmth and movement beside me as we shuffled through the dry leaves. Where he grew up, what he did as a kid, where he went to school, his hobbies, his friends, the fishing trip he took with his brother every spring, everything we shared, including my dream of being a doctor some day or my memories of growing up in my home town, made the magic circle bigger, drew its power closer.

Robbinsdale didn't seem so bleak any more. Ever since my family had moved here from the Iron Range five years earlier, I had felt sad; it seemed my whole family felt sad – it hung over us like the dark tones in those old photographs of my mother's. We had left so much behind: our friends, our roots, our connection with familiar streets and neighborhoods, the lakes and woods of the North Country. The suburbs were block after block of tract housing; hills were leveled, swamps filled in, the places where you could play grew fewer and smaller with every passing year. In the compact city of Virginia, rimmed on the north by the huge open-pit iron mines of the Mesabi, I had free rein; I ran with the Gregorich kids through fields and woods, roamed the neighborhoods of the south and west side, walked downtown for a pop or an ice cream cone. One afternoon I had waved to Grandma strolling on the other side of main street with her friend Lottie; on a winter afternoon, I had come across my Aunt Ginny carrying her ice skates over her shoulder on the way to the rink near our house. But Robbinsdale was different; it was nestled in a ring of suburbs surrounding a huge city. It was full of rules and places that were off-limits, and my aunt and grandma – who had moved down at the same time as us, three generations all living in the same house for more than a year – now lived several miles away, in opposite directions; there was no running into them any more, only Sunday visits. Everybody felt disconnected here, and we were still strangers after five years. Spring didn't smell as sweet, snow fell with less sparkle, and the deep red of roses only reminded me of summers long gone.

Yet walking home with Mr. Hanson night after night, I was happy. I forgot the silly game I played on the way home from school when I was by myself, not stepping on any lines or cracks in the sidewalk. "Step on a crack, break your mother's back; step on a line, break your mother's spine." That was kid stuff. This new world

I was on the threshold of entering was filled, not with fear and superstition, but promise and possibility. The evidence was all around me, not locked away in some dreamy, idealized past, not slipping away forever out of reach. It was here and now, present in the night air, sweet and pungent with the smell of wood fires and burning leaves; in the snug houses breathing forth their welcoming aromas of pot roast and apple pie; in the warm yellow glow of the window panes dancing like lanterns strung in the jagged tree branches... and in the man walking here beside me.

Seventh grade didn't seem so threatening any more. Jakes' bullying was already becoming a thing of the past; I could handle gym – only two more years; and I could learn what was expected of me, how to act, how to fit in. The world was intelligible, manageable.

Then one night, just before the Thanksgiving holiday, something strange happened. We were walking home as usual. It was chilly, and a wet snow matted the leaves and made them stick to our shoes. I'm not sure what I said, if anything – I was always so careful – but perhaps I let myself get too excited and talkative, too happy; that was always a danger. Probably the pieces suddenly fit together for Mr. Hanson, for half-way home he stopped short and looked at me, as if a light bulb had switched on inside his head.

"Why, you're a little fruit, aren't you."

Memory stops. What went through my head? Did I think, maybe I didn't hear him right? Surely, he couldn't be saying these words to me. What did they mean anyway? I wasn't a fruit or a fairy or anything like that. I just liked helping him and walking home with him. As he spoke those words, the signal must have faded fast, like bad radio reception. I imagine that dazed astonishment quickly gave way to puzzlement, then to blankness, before the signal ceased entirely.

I felt nothing. Nothing then, nothing on the rest of the walk home, nothing in my room that night, nothing at school the next day or in the months and years to come. Not sadness or disappointment; not anger, hurt or loss; not betrayal, humiliation or fear. Nothing, until years later when I came out and started to heal. The emotional record is a total blank, but the historical record is clear: I stopped walking home with him, stopped helping him clean up after class, stopped prowling the halls to catch a glimpse of him.

I confess I am in awe of that boy. In many ways he is, and always will be, a stranger to me. Try as I might, I cannot retrieve or re-create who he was or what he felt at that unique moment in his history, but his strength, self-possession and sheer survival power amaze me. Even at that tender age, he is already so strong that almost nothing can touch him. Yet for years, I couldn't touch him either. That boy, who had begun to taste hope and love and freedom, who had begun tentatively to emerge, was driven inward, to a recess of privacy so deep, that for years he was totally lost to me.

Wet Dream

When I started to come out, and was torn by fear, excitement, self-doubt and possibility, I confided my secret to a comfortably out gay man at work. Perhaps he could help me in this process.

He shared with me a sexual dream he had had when he was twelve or thirteen that convinced him once and for all that he was gay. Excited and aroused by the dream – I think it was about a shop teacher – he was able to conclude something important about himself without much prior thought or experience, or much deliberation afterward. The dream was all he needed.

Dreams don't lie, he thought to himself. He might fool himself in his waking life, by explaining away or denying his feelings, but not while he slept. He took the dream, in all its clarity, as a talisman on his coming-out journey. Jon, at twenty-six, was a well-adjusted gay man, emotionally and politically aware, in a stable and committed, if unconventional, relationship. He struggled with all the career and life issues typical of a man in his twenties, but in a context of healthy self-acceptance. He knew who he was.

I too had had a telling dream when I was 12 or 13. I was sleeping on the couch at my aunt's, keeping her company during a painful divorce. In my dream I am waiting with a crowd of people outside an elevator high up in a modernistic office building, like something you might see in the movies. Expectant, excited, we are awaiting the arrival of someone important. The doors open and out steps the most beautiful man I have ever seen, naked, but with a body of light, radiant and translucent. The figure is dazzling. I think it must be Jesus.

I wake with a wet spot on my pajamas. I make no connection between the dream and the wet spot; I don't even know what the wet spot means. I make no connection between the dream and my feelings about men. I make no connections whatsoever. The system of denial is already intact, and the dream remains an anomaly.

The Call

"Hello, is this Robert, Robert Anderson, who used to live on Quail Avenue?" said a husky female voice with a New York accent.

"Yeah," I answered sleepily – it was way past my bedtime.

"This is Linda, Robert, Linda Margolis. I've been trying to reach you – you wouldn't believe how many Robert Andersons there are in Minneapolis! I finally remembered your brother's name, and that's how I found you. I'm afraid I woke him too."

"Oh, yeah, hi, it's been a long time."

She launched into a breathless explanation, which I could barely follow, something about a skull with a gold piece in its eye socket that she had found one day in a pawn shop on New York's Lower East Side and knew she had to have it because it reminded her of the stories I had told her when we were kids growing up next door to each other in Robbinsdale.

"Do you remember the stories about The Torch and the Black Castle?"

"Sure, how could I forget."

"Well, I'm sitting working at my desk and suddenly the skull tumbles off the bookshelf with a terrible clatter and rolls toward my feet, where it stops, staring up at me. I knew it was a sign, I had to call."

"Wow, no wonder."

Her voice was richer than I remembered it, smoky with undertones, layered with life, but familiar still after all those years. It tripped memory, and suddenly I saw the girl of nine or ten, with her pretty oval face and large inquisitive brown eyes, a tuft of dark brown hair clumped like a palm tree that spilled down the back of her head. Her pale forearms were webbed with a delicate tracery of dark silken hair. It might as well have been yesterday that we spent hot summer afternoons sitting on the cool mossy grass on the secluded north side of the house on Quail.

"I liked making up those stories," I said. "You were skeptical at first, real sharp for so young a kid, but in the end, you bought 'em, hook, line and sinker."

"Robert, when I moved, I clung to those stories. They were what kept me going when I felt so sad and lost about everything that I had left behind."

"You're kidding. For me, it was just a lark."

"I can't believe that," she said. "Those stories were magical."

I hadn't seen Linda for close to fifteen years, not since we had bumped into each other as students at the University of Minnesota. I was one or two years ahead of her. Then, we had exchanged pleasantries and caught up on history. She had moved away from the neighborhood some ten years earlier, and we had kept in touch for awhile as kids, then drifted apart. Now, I heard a tale of a childhood spent in mourning, grieving a lost world of enchantment, of which I had been the unwitting magus.

"You won't believe the time I've spent in therapy! I should send you the bill!" We laughed. "I don't know why, but when I moved away, it was like my life split in two. I didn't have any friends, I didn't fit in or feel connected. I brooded on my unhappiness and took refuge in my memories of Robbinsdale, those stories, and you. So many times in therapy, no matter what I was dealing with, career or relationships, it all came back to that. I think I've got it sorted out now, and maybe that's why I'm calling – to let go."

She was letting all this go? I confess I took a perverse pride in my influence on her life; I even boasted of it the next day at work. It was hard to believe that such a competent woman as Linda – a successful, self-employed fundraiser for multimillion-dollar projects – could in any way be seriously hampered by anything so remote and miniscule as a few stories from childhood.

"Do you remember the secret passageway from the root cellar in your basement to the Black Castle? Do you remember the time you had Ronnie dress up like The Torch to convince me the whole thing wasn't a scam?"

"Yeah, and you suspected it was Ronnie, and I had to cook up another scheme. What I remember is how hard you were to convince of anything. When I showed you the picture of the Black Castle, which I had drawn, then baked the paper in the oven and burnt the edges with a match, swabbing it in cobwebs to make it look old, you said, 'This looks like Sleeping Beauty's castle from the movie ads.' You were one shrewd cookie."

For years afterward, more than I care to admit, I had kept a folder labeled, in florid Gothic lettering, "The Torch," containing the memorabilia associated with this prank, until one day it too was consigned to the dustbin of history, like all the other relics of childhood. I had invented an elaborate tale, doled out in snippets to my eager auditor, that combined elements from the Brothers Grimm, Walt Disney, old horror movies, bowdlerized Poe and Cold War intrigue, somehow all fused together thanks to an overactive imagination. Was it all a con, or did I half-believe it myself? For Linda, the fascination with the fantastic had remained. Her life was filled with strange coincidences and psychic experiences. She had recently toured the Mongolian desert on horseback, accompanied only by a native guide, in search of the land and legends out of which her distant ancestors had sprung before settling in Russia. The eyes of her guide had haunted her, until one day she realized what it was and snapped a photograph of him to send to her mother. "Where on earth did you get that shot of your father as a young man? – I've never seen it," her mother had said.

She filled me in on her life, and it didn't sound happy – an abusive relationship, the death of her brother's wife shortly after marriage, her mother's long illness. Surely there was a statute of limitations on childhood pranks.

"I'm amazed you remember all that stuff from so long ago, and that it still means so much to you," I said. "I don't feel any connection with it any more – it's just the detritus of childhood."

"That can't possibly be true, you couldn't have left it all behind."

"Well, I did. I'm a married man, I've got a five-year-old daughter, a home in the suburbs, a job as an editor. There's plenty on my plate without all that stuff from the past."

"It's got to be there somewhere," she said.

"Nope, I'm just a regular guy, terribly ordinary, boring in fact. Right now I'm working hard to finish my dissertation so I can get my Ph.D. and teach literature, which is what I really want to do."

"What's your thesis on?," she asked.

"Alfred Lord Tennyson, Victorian literature, his poem, 'The Holy Grail' – it's part of the *Idylls of the King*. I'm looking at it in the context of 19th-century theories of mythopoesis, how the poet re-invents and re-interprets the ancient myth for his own age. Most people would consider it a little dry, but I like it."

"Don't you see, there it is, right in front of you, the boy who made up the magical stories."

"You gotta be kidding – this is serious stuff." I had to admit, there were some interesting correspondences, now that she mentioned it, between the mysterious, fabulous quest for the grail and its secret of eternal life, and those wild tales I told her so many years ago, but that was just a coincidence. What had my serious study of literature, my concern with questions of form and art and literary criticism, to do with childish make-believe?

"I'd hate to think that boy was lost. I liked him. You said you were an editor."

"I work for an occult book publishing company in St. Paul. Llewellyn. We do books, magazines, operate a wholesale and retail outlet, provide astrological consulting services via mail, the whole shebang. I work with astrologers, palmists, Tarot readers, witches, warlocks, magicians – that's magick with a k, not the white-bunny-in-the-hat stuff. Beelzebub, the 32nd Degree, Crossing the Abyss. It's a blast!"

"I hate to say it, Robert, but there it is again."

"Naw, I don't believe in any of that stuff. It's just a job. In some ways I wish I were more open to it, there's got to be something to it. But I'm the wrong guy. I just went through all those years of college, have blasted my brains studying for my Ph.D., and the last bit of magical thinking was wrung out of me years ago."

"That's too bad," she said.

"You should have seen my job interview. I was interrogated by the publisher in this creepy old mansion on Summit Avenue, a certified haunted house on a national registry, and I'm looking at him and on the wall behind him, a photograph of his face lit from below by a candle , throwing everything into spooky relief, his grey mane and beard, and those bulgy Pisces fish eyes of his staring down at me – you see, I'm even starting to talk like them. A few days earlier I had filled out a six-page single space job application form, and I had to list all the books I had ever read that had anything to do with the occult. I wracked my brain and came up with quite a list: William Blake, Swedenborg, Yeats's *A Vision*. I hadn't even read them all, but I needed the job. Wouldn't you know, he started quizzing me about Yeats's cyclical theory of history and its correspondence with astrology. It was like taking my goddam prelims all over again."

She laughed. "How did you do?"

"Fine. After nearly twelve years of college, if you count the years of part-time teaching, and twenty-four years of schooling total, if you count grade school and high school, I can ace any exam. Then – you won't believe this – after he finishes, he calls for this guy who descends a grand staircase, a giant of a man, at least six-foot-six, an opera singer who plays Wotan in the "Ring" cycle – Noel Tyl. I had just read about him the night before while proofreading copy for the *Minnesota Daily*. What a creepy coincidence. I'm supposed to edit his twelve-volume college text on the principles and practice of astrology, and he's got a say in the hiring. He's been upstairs, in one of the turrets, casting my solar chart based on the info in my application, and he proceeds to tell Carl everything about me, like how I need to work independently without too much supervision because of all the planets retrograde in my something-or-other. And you know, he's got me pegged, it's like he knows me, and Carl listens to every word, and Presto!, I'm hired."

"What I want to know is, did this mansion look anything like the Black Castle?" I laughed. "Robert, remember, 'The child is the father of the man.'"

"Wordsworth. 'Intimations' ode. 1802, I think."

"That's not the point. Where have you been all your life, that you feel no connection with that boy? Maybe I've been sent to you for a reason – I've kept him in trust for you all these years."

I felt a twinge of sadness, which I quickly discounted. Why wasn't I more receptive to the wacky adventure at Llewellyn? But that was only symptomatic. Why wasn't I more open to life and people generally? I was aloof, on guard, always the critic, detached and superior, analyzing, evaluating, judging, dismissing, putting life at a distance. Whether it was the past or the present, my own life or someone else's, in every sphere of thought and endeavor, it was the same – I felt a fundamental disconnect. If I was a specimen under glass, so was Linda, so was the whole world.

It happened in an instant, below consciousness, this opening and closing of feeling. Sadness gave way to bitterness, which in turn was quickly subsumed in smug resignation. Of course, being an adult was difficult – nobody claimed otherwise. It meant sacrifice, compromise, the acceptance of limitation and inevitable disappointment. The machinery worked like a charm; everything clicked into place; the defenses and rationalizations worn smooth with years of habitual use took over, and I was on familiar ground again, comfortable if chilling, the arid plain of my emptiness and discontent. Better this than sadness. This I could dress up in the intellectual trappings of existential courage. If I tapped that other vein, who knew where the pain might lead.

I was tired, and we ended the conversation, but not before I invited her to have dinner with my wife and daughter and me the next time she was in town visiting her parents. She would see how ordinary we were; maybe it would do her good; reality was bracing. But in my heart of hearts, I hoped she wouldn't be too disillusioned. I treasured the fact that once, long ago, that boy had held her under his spell.

The Bargain

I had struck a bargain in my late teens. It's a temptation when we're in crisis. We trade something of value that we possess, for something else we desire. Do we get more than we lose? I traded the boy; I wanted peace of mind.

No more running up the basement stairs in a sweating terror, no more hiding my head under the covers at night so I wouldn't see the faces congealing like gargoyles in the dark corners near the ceiling, no more visions of God in the moon, beautiful and terrible at the same time. No more dreaming or make-believe or yearning for the unattainable. No more openness or vulnerability. Imagination and impressionability had their cost. If my growing up was full of fear and insecurity, fueled in part by a dread of discovery, and if on the threshold of adulthood I found myself stranded in a loneliness so intense, I felt alien, the solution was simple: disown it all.

The groundwork had already been laid. The sell-out of that boy had begun years before, with the keeping of secrets, the lies, the cultivation of an inner life inherently unsharable with any other living soul. That boy, with his hypnotic mantras on the way to school, his deliberate erections, was too clever for his own good. If, by the time of his late teens, he was so skilled in his games and subterfuges, so adept at compartmentalizing his feelings, that he lost track of what he truly felt and thought, and got trapped in a maze of his own making, did he have anyone to blame but himself? I, the responsible adult, only hammered the last nails in the coffin.

With almost palpable relief, I seized the tools handed to me in college. It was a revelation. Ah, I thought, this is how it's done, this is how you make sense of the world, escape the impotence and insecurity of childhood. Knowledge, the wisdom of the ages, the truths of science and reason, the tools of logic and analysis – with these I would fashion a surrogate reality, and it would be factual, rational, manageable, and above all, out there, anywhere but in here, and tainted by me. "The life of the mind," "the examined life," "the life of reason" – I could glorify it and give it many names, but at bottom, for me, it was a bit of a dodge.

Linda was right. There, masked in the dedicated scholar pouring over the sacred texts of literature, spinning his subtle webs of interpretive theory, lurked the boy, the yarn-spinning spellbinder of Robbinsdale, who long ago had sat with her on the cool mossy grass and charmed her childhood irredeemably with tales of magic and intrigue.

I loved college, every bit of it, from hitting the books at all hours and wrestling with a subject till I knew it inside and out, to demonstrating mastery in papers and exams. I inhabited the library like a second home, stealing cat-naps face-down on interlocked arms, my nose tucked in the gutter of a book, breathing in its heady vapors of glue, paper and ink. I couldn't tear myself away, not even for lunch; I'd park in some out-of-the-way corner of the art library and surreptitiously gobble down my peanut butter and jelly sandwiches while drinking in the gorgeous pages of the Skira art books – Breughel, Bosch, Klee, Chagall – being careful to turn the pages with my knuckles or pinky finger so as not to smudge the plates. In this rarefied, hermetic atmosphere, I flourished, came into my own. I had never been happier.

It didn't come easily, however. I almost bombed out during my first quarter at the university, getting a D in Freshman English – writing, my best subject. As in seventh grade, the rules were changing, but this time in my favor; success didn't depend on decoding sexual signals. I was bright, inquisitive and serious-minded; all I needed was someone to show me the ropes... and I found him in my second quarter of Freshman English.

Burton Jasper Weber was a scholar, a critic with a passion for literature, and a man who viewed teaching as an almost ministerial vocation. Souls were at stake in the clunky sentences of student themes, and in the refining fire of composition, they were made or lost. I may have drifted through my life up till then, but no longer; he saw talent, and called me to accounts.

I was serious about school this quarter and determined to get a good grade in English. I worked hard on my first theme, taking it through several drafts, even enlisting the help of my father, a journalism major in college. When Mr. Weber was ready to hand back our first assignment, I waited expectantly all through class.

"Needs work" was all he muttered as he thrust the paper toward me without raising his eyes. I scanned the pages quickly, looking everywhere for the grade, then turned them over, skimming past four pages of commentary he had meticulously written in an eccentric script, a hurried hybrid of cursive and printed letters, with small x's marking the ends of sentences. His comments were as long as the theme itself, and there at the end glared the impossible grade: D– over F++. I hadn't quite failed.

Outside in the hall, as my grumbling classmates filed past, I leaned against the wall, my breathing fast and high in my chest, my heart pounding, my hands shaking, reading and rereading the blur in front of me till it crystallized and I began to break the code. What emerged was a dismal chronicle of every flaw in logic and organization, every lapse of unity and coherence, every instance of an unexamined assumption or unsupported generalization. Forget the niceties of spelling, punctuation and grammar – that was kid stuff; these were essential failings of thinking and lucidity, perception and understanding. I felt as if my very being were on trial. I was furious; I hated this man, this skinny martinet with his ramrod posture, always dressed in grays and blacks, his endless pacing back and forth in front of us, his harangues, his righteous indignation not only with our moral and intellectual failings – we freshmen, after all, were only the tip of the iceberg – but the vast venality and corruption of the culture at large. He thundered judgment like an Old Testament prophet.

Later, as I met the members of my carpool at Coffman Union, sprawled lazily in the fat easy chairs of the men's lounge, I paced back and forth in front of them, waving the pages of my theme in the air, denouncing this petty classroom tyrant, defending my paper and arguing with every one of his points. That argument continued for weeks, theme after theme, rewrite after rewrite (we could redo a paper as often as we wanted to improve the grade). With every revision, I wrote back long, angry counter-arguments, as detailed as his commentaries, and he replied on the reverse side, calmly, deliberately, saying I had missed the point. Through all the back-and-forth, grudgingly, gradually, I kept making changes, till I got it right: my thesis statements became more pointed and defensible, my organization clearer and more logically related to my thesis, my development more thorough, relevant and rational. Like Sisyphus pushing his rock up the hill, my grades crept up his skewed curve – D, D++ over C–, C++ over B–, B, B+ over A–, A–, A, A++. I wasn't arguing any more. I was in awe of this man, his staying power, his patience with me, his belief in my ability, his essential rightness and integrity. And I felt he had given me an immeasurable gift: he had shown me how to use my mind.

And I learned how to read literature. I had always loved reading, and both my parents were avid readers. Our house was full of books. For most of the years of my growing up, my dad kept the Modern Library edition of Thoreau's *Walden* open at his bedside, turned face-down to mark where he had left off the night before. I couldn't imagine why he never finished the book; after Mr. Weber, I knew. As a kid, I'd regularly trek the seven blocks to the old Tudor-style library on the edge of downtown – in the fall kicking up piles of leaves in the gutters – each time returning home with a precious stack of books cradled precariously in my arms. In junior high, my dad cultivated this interest by buying me "Classics Illustrated" comic books, weaning me from "Superman," "Archie" and "Scrooge McDuck," and it's here that I first encountered *Gulliver's Travels, Robinson Crusoe* and *The Hunchback of*

Notre Dame. He was whetting a taste for the real thing, which he dutifully supplied all through high school, bringing me classics from the library like *Moby Dick, Les Miserables* and *The Great Gatsby.* These I curled up with every night before going to sleep, losing myself in the sort of waking dream that only the spell of words can evoke.

I already had the taste for good literature. What Mr. Weber supplied was a deepening of my appreciation, the understanding and skill to identify and analyze why these books moved me, and the ability and confidence to communicate that persuasively to others. In addition, at a time when I felt beneath notice, he recognized my gifts and gave them his imprimatur, telling me that they were of value in this world... that I was of value.

After my final exam – an analysis of John Crowe Ransom's poem, "Dead Boy," an elegy on the death of a scion of a southern family – he wrote me a postcard, in that curious script of his, encouraging me to pursue the study of literature. I have it still, tucked in the pages of my confirmation Bible, more than 40 years later, now yellowed and frayed with age, its penciled print barely legible any longer. But I know it by heart; it ends with the words, "You've got promise."

How ironic, I think now – "Dead Boy," my ticket to a new life. Mr. Weber became my mentor, then my friend. He guided me through my undergraduate education, steering me toward the best, and most demanding, courses and teachers. Through him, I learned to appreciate classical music, Danish modern furniture, metaphysical poetry, hand-crafted jewelry, ethnic and gourmet cooking. With him playing matchmaker, I met the woman who would become my wife. And inspired by his example, I did the unthinkable: I became a teacher.

I didn't know what I wanted to be when I entered college, but one thing I knew for certain: I didn't want to be a teacher. The thought of standing in front of a group of people and presuming to any knowledge or authority repelled and terrified me. What did such fears matter, however, what did gut instinct or basic creature comfort matter, when weighed against so noble a calling, so inspiring an example? I was on a bold adventure, reinventing myself. Ding-dong, the fearful boy was dead.

This transformation, however, proved as difficult as learning to write a decent composition. First, I had to be lured out of my self-protective isolation. It was my sophomore year, I was still living at home with my parents, and the professional, then mentoring relationship with Mr. Weber was gradually blurring into a friendship. He had taken to inviting me to dinner with him and his wife, a former student of his. I'd be raking the yard, sitting under the apple tree reading Wordsworth or Donne, or typing a paper on my dad's Olympia typewriter, and I'd get the fleeting thought, a twinge really, Shouldn't I be calling Mr. Weber, hadn't it been a month or so since we last talked? Invariably, he'd call first, with yet another invitation. I rarely took social initiative with anyone. And just as invariably, I'd feel guilty. I was a poor friend, and for Mr. Weber, friendship was a supreme value. I wasn't sure how I viewed these visits. I was flattered, of course, but also puzzled. What did I have to offer? As the date approached, I'd get anxious; I'd bone up, rehearsing topics of conversation, clever remarks, the parts of my life it was safe to disclose. I had to be equal to the task. For Mr. Weber, conversation was an art, and it meant more than sharing observations and ideas. If its highest reaches were speculations on the nature of the True, the Good and the

Beautiful, the ground was intimacy, the sharing of feelings and perceptions, stories about family and friends. Now I was accountable not only for how I used my talents, but for who I was. I was drawn out, in spite of myself, and in the process, I both discovered and created myself.

Somehow, through all my nervousness and studied manner, something appealing must have shone through, for the invitations kept coming. My interest in art, philosophy, liberal politics and literature were all genuine, as were my enthusiasm and idealism. Once I managed to shed my skittishness, and relax into the stuffy atmosphere of his small apartment, I drank it all in, the quick wit, the play of ideas, the impassioned rhetoric, even the scathing indictments of human nature and American culture. This world had a certain clarity and integrity to it, and everything was charged with meaning; nothing was accidental or ambiguous. From the food on the table to the art on the walls, from the sleek Dansk furniture to the stern moral pronouncements, it was all of a piece, a way of life, everything bespeaking standards of taste and judgment.

In other words, the opposite of my life. In eighth grade my art teacher had asked each of us to prepare an oral report on the architecture and decor of our home, including a description of our dream house. For years afterward, my parents had chuckled at my characterization of our decor, with its hodge-podge of hand-me-down furniture and upended orange crates covered with green plastic skirts serving as end tables. "Early Salvation Army," I had called it. Burton laughed too, when I related this story over our meal of vichyssoise and braised calve's tongue, not affectionately like my parents, but with an air of contempt – and I knew he was right. I was ready to chuck it all.

Over the next many months, his tiny apartment, with its heady bouquet of pipe tobacco smoke, clean sweat and dusty books, came to signify for me everything that was needed for the good life. The rooms were honeycombed with books, newspapers, magazines and classical records – every available surface and cubbyhole stacked and stuffed with treasures. These I thumbed through, borrowed and pressed into service when conversation flagged; after all, I had only so much material to share. Better to read and comment on Dr. Johnson's attack on the fideist conservative Soame Jenyns, or peruse the Earl of Rochester's banned erotic verse. Burton seemed to possess every hidden gem of English literature. Better to spend the evening listening to his extensive record collection, over the latest in hi-fi equipment; two electrostatic speakers, more than five feet high, made the harpsichord in Bach's "Italian Concerto" sound as if it were present in the center of the room. Sometimes we'd listen to an entire opera: *Don Giovanni, The Rake's Progress, Peter Grimes, Salome*. These dinners were six-hour marathons – total immersion. I'd come home thrilled and exhausted, my mind buzzing, unable to sleep, drunk on consciousness... and all that beauty.

It was a seduction of sorts, and I was ripe for the taking. Don't get me wrong, none of this was homoerotic. My attraction to Burton depended entirely on what he represented; its power derived precisely from its ability to neutralize and subsume the whole problem of sex. It helped that Burton was a man of supreme moral rectitude, and that I was so serenely, and deliberately, innocent. In books and music and art, in conversation about people and ideas, I could explore love and passion and sex – anything I wanted, the entire human condition – but at a comfortable remove, outside myself, filtered through the lens of a controlling consciousness. In projecting my feelings and perceptions, my yearnings and imaginings, my questions and life struggles, onto the great works of western culture, I heightened and transformed my predicament, I merged with something larger than myself, both losing and finding myself at the same time. By following Burton's example, and explicating the moral schema underlying the dramatic structure in James's *The Portrait of a Lady* or Shakespeare's *Twelfth Night*, I could explore and refine my own taste and judgment, shape and articulate my own aesthetic and moral sensibility. If for John Keats, life was a "vale of soul-making," art would be mine. It was a grand project, and I embraced it with my whole being.

In my junior year I adopted Burton as my "spiritual father." That's exactly what I called him, with all the hubris of youth. Implicit, I knew, was a disowning of my own father. What did mere biology or blood history matter when weighed against so exalted a project?

It all sounds too clear and deliberate laid out this way. We do create a persona for ourselves, an identity, a mask that we present to ourselves and others to define our role in the world; it is both a revelation and a concealment, a means of engaging the world, and of defending against it. The process is largely unconscious. If there is a fog of war, out of which events and outcomes materialize, there is a fog of identity as well; out of the confusion of adolescence, we stumble into adulthood. In a process that is half exploration and half creation, half accident and half intention, we discover and bring to birth certain potentialities in ourselves, while shadowing or minimizing others. We become this, instead of that. In part, that's the way it was for me as well, but intention played the greater role. It had to. There was something of the studied and grandiose in my renunciation of childhood, my adoption of Burton, my re-invention of myself. Given my predicament, however, what was the alternative?

Burton was no Svengali. He did not create me; I created me... after his fashion. He only provided a way out of a painful dilemma. What could I do with the dreamy boy of my childhood if I had to kill him to survive? I could transmute him.

One day late in my freshman year Denny Nelson stopped to offer me a ride as I walked home from the bus. I hadn't seen him since high school, but we had long since drifted apart. Our last time together had been that day he had told me how wonderful the love of a woman was, and how he hoped I would know it some day. I had felt so close to him that afternoon – how close, I would realize only years later – but as I sat next to him in the car, I felt no connection with him. It was as if that afternoon, our friendship, our growing up together in the same neighborhood all those years had never happened. I must have been full of myself, for I talked about nothing but Mr. Weber this and Mr. Weber that, what a wonderful teacher he was, how much I was learning and how my life was transformed. Denny couldn't get a word in edgewise. His parting shot as I left the car was, "You're stuck up." Maybe in high school these words might have stung, but what did they matter now? They were from another world. They couldn't touch me – nothing could.

MARRIAGE

Courtship

Of all the students Burton cultivated as friends over the years – and they were many, mostly women, and usually troubled – I'm one of the few who really took. One of those women became his wife; another would become mine.

Judy was a year behind me in college and was taking his Freshman English class when I sat in to hear his lectures on *King Lear*. She was his brightest student, he said, and she was having trouble at home with her parents. "Maybe you'd enjoy meeting her, and she could certainly use a friend right now," he said. A few weeks later he asked if he could invite her to join us for dinner some evening.

"Sure, why not?," I said with a sinking feeling in my gut. Yet how could I refuse? It felt posed as a moral choice, like everything in Burton's universe.

In memory that meeting is a blank except for some vague impressions: stuffy apartment, me hot and cramped sitting in my Danish modern chair after eating too much rich food, leaning forward and straining to hear and take in this strange new person who sits in the chair opposite me. The one clear presence in the room, making his pronouncements while pacing back and forth in front of us, dividing the room into smaller and smaller segments, is Burton – mentor, mediator, impresario of the evening. I take comfort in that presence, the way balanced and antithetical gestures of arms and hands mirror the intricate process of thought, the weighing of evidence, the assignment of value and judgment. If this strange new world I am on the verge of entering feels ambiguous and fraught with unspoken expectations, is it anything other than the world I relish encountering in literature, and could I ask for a better guide than Burton?

I'd been here before. In high school my Aunt Virginia had set me up with this "really sweet girl – she'll be just right for you." I dodged or laughed off her suggestions as long as I could but she was a relentless godmother, intent on discharging her duties, and eventually invited Lois and me over to her house one evening, got us seated on the couch in front of the TV, then after some pleasantries, excused herself, shutting the door behind her – "so you'll have some privacy," she said. For what? I didn't date, had no interest in girls, and since boys were strictly off-limits, the whole issue of desire was moot, relegated to the realm of dreamy fantasy. I squirmed and sweated, didn't know what to do with my hands, babbled about school and philosophy and stared dully at the TV waiting for a graceful exit line. I knew something was expected of me, that failure to deliver meant I was deficient as a man, and beneath lurked darker, unnamable fears.

I met John Kelly about the same time I met Judy, though I didn't realize this till many years later, upon reflection. In my mind the two stories barely occupy the same universe, much less happen to the same person. He belongs to that other life of mine.

I first see him lolling in his chair at the end of a row, illuminated in the bright sunlight that floods in from the tall open window behind me. I sit on its broad ledge, a late registrant in an overcrowded classroom, hoping to make the cut in this, my inaugural English class. The crisp fall air is pungent with the promise of a new school year, but this is even more exciting: he is unbelievably handsome. I rivet my gaze, glad I sit off to the side where I can watch with impunity.

Professor Buckley is droning on about the vagaries of university administration while taking inventory of his surplus population, and I note carefully the name of this man as he calls the roll: "Kelly, John." The professor, who talks through puckered lips as if he has sucked too long on the lemon of life, is making lame jokes about the crisis in the Congo and the race between Nixon and Kennedy, but this guy is smiling, and it's the smile that gets me. It's with his whole face, his head cocked and a slight forward thrust of his upper body – broad, toothy, generous, a Kennedy smile bestowed like a benediction upon the world.

What have I missed in the professor's remarks? I try to concentrate but I'm distracted. Close-cropped dark hair, with flecks of gray at the temples; a boyish face, curious and intelligent, with keen blue eyes crinkling at the corners with impish amusement; pale cheeks with the faintest blush of beard, which deepens along the upper lip, throwing its curves into tender relief; full chest and shoulders; furry forearms; legs in polished chinos stretched out and crossed at the ankles, shiny penny loafers – I take the trip again and again, as often as I think I can get away with it. He leans forward, relaxes back, taps the eraser tip of the pencil against his front teeth, then hunches down to write, cradling his head in the crook of his elbow, totally absorbed in his thoughts.

Again, I've missed something – early literary influences, I think – and I scramble to jot something, anything down. But like filings to a magnet, my attention reverts to the man at the end of the row. What draws me, moves me, more than his face or figure, is his bearing, a certain attitude or gesture toward the world: confident, relaxed, engaged.

I make the cut, and can't believe my good fortune when several days later I discover him riding home on my bus. I muscle my way to the back, muttering excuses to the students clogging the aisle.

"Hi, you're in my sophomore survey class." He looks up from his book. Joyce's *The Dubliners* – I have the same edition.

"Oh yeah?"

"I noticed you the first day, I even remember your name from when the professor called the roll. John Kelly, right?"

"That's really something." That smile.

"My name's Bob Anderson. This is my first English class. I live in Robbinsdale." To my delight I discover that's where he lives, in a rented room he shares with an Army buddy whose music director at Elim Lutheran, my aunt's church! He's 26, Irish Catholic and a native of Long Island where his family attends the same church as Perry Como. He sang all over Europe in the Army chorus, has taken other English classes and is a devotee of the writers of the Irish Renaissance.

"Most people don't know how many of the great

English authors are really Irish," he says. "Not just Joyce and Yeats and Wilde, but Shaw and Swift and Goldsmith." I suck up the facts like a vacuum cleaner. I hang on his every word as I'm jostled by the students shoving to get off the bus, and bumped up and down and tossed side to side as the bus lurches from stop to stop.

From that day forward I never mount the bus without looking for him, craning my neck and peering over and around the crowd in the aisle to check every single seat. Occasionally these efforts are rewarded with another conversation, and then I ride home happy; but on those cold grey days when there's no sign of him, I watch at every stop, my nose and forehead glued and bumping against the glass, my hopes rising and falling with every block.

Through these conversations a casual intimacy grows. On the day I learn his middle name is Thaddeus, I know I have been granted a great confidence indeed; and on another trip, when he declines to tell me why he joined and then left the Christian Brothers, alluding to a breakdown and a hospital stay – "I don't talk about that with anyone," he says – I take the prohibition reverentially. I ponder all these things, stash every fact away in my growing trove of knowledge and begin to make these encounters more than accidental. I learn that he subscribes to the Friday night symphony and adjust my schedule accordingly.

Given our inauspicious beginning, how was it that Judy and I got acquainted? I'm sure we chatted from time to time after Burton's class, and when I stopped attending, she must have suggested a play or movie some afternoon followed by dinner at a Dinkytown restaurant, for I remember her taking off her jacket after she was seated, and the light above the booth shining down on a pretty turquoise mohair top, accentuating the gentle curve of her breasts. I gasped, and she asked what was wrong. "Nothing," I said. It's one of two times in my life when I recall an involuntary visceral response to the beauty of a woman.

After too much time had passed, my mother reminded me, "What about that nice girl you went out with?," and Burton too joined the chorus: "What do you hear from Judy?" and later, "How are things going with her parents?"

Eventually Judy began turning up in the oddest places, like in the mornings when my dad dropped me off near the Washington Avenue bridge where I crossed to get to my classes. On cold wintry days, with the wind whipping down the frozen Mississippi, that crossing could be nasty. What a pleasant surprise, then, on one of those mornings to find Judy parked at the foot of the bridge, her cozy green Valiant purring welcome. "I saw you walking, thought you might like a ride."

"You bet, thanks a lot." Funny, I thought as I hopped in, I don't remember telling her how I got to school. This happened more than once, then she started turning up even on warm sunny days. "Just happened to be passing through and thought I'd wait a few minutes to see if you'd crossed yet. It's a nice day, so if you'd rather walk, that's O.K." What a lucky break, I thought; I was getting to like these times together.

When the school year ended, we didn't see each other that summer except for one crazy bike ride I took out to her house in Edina. It was a hot, humid afternoon and I rode the ten or twelve miles on a shoulder beside

Highway 100 with no helmet and the cars whizzing past me from the rear. I arrived sweaty and out of breath, barely able to talk at first; I could only stay an hour, I said, and despite rush hour I insisted on biking back, ignoring her pleas to let her drive me home. It was a grandiose gesture, this heroic ride of mine, perfect and self-contained, admitting of no possibility of real intimacy, but in its high drama more than compensating, I hoped, for all the slights and silences of the past few months.

Meanwhile, I was getting quite an education in classical music. Sometimes I rode home cold and lonely after the symphony, but twice I managed to catch up with John and was ecstatic when he proposed lunch. The conversation that noon flowed, witty, silly and thoughtful by turns, touching on nearly everything I was studying and thinking about – poetry, drama, music, politics, philosophy – but here in this man, lived and breathed as part of the texture of his ordinary personal life, not rarefied and intellectualized as it sometimes seemed with Burton... and nearly always was with me.

The following quarter we didn't have the same class. Occasionally I'd spot him on the mall or in the halls of Folwell and then, no matter what my destination, I'd do an about-face and tag along, happy as a puppy to be at his side. On one of those walks we were discussing the relative merits of Plato and Aristotle.

"I'm a Platonist," he said.

"What do you mean?" I was studying Plato's *Republic* in my political theory class, but here was a living, breathing Platonist. It must be something he picked up from the Christian Brothers.

"This is a world of appearances only," he said.

"We don't see things for what they really are. The truth lies beyond. Here we see as through a glass darkly." Paul, I thought, not Plato.

"I don't know, you look plenty real to me. I wouldn't like to think I lived only in a world of shadows. It sounds too life-denying to me, Jack." He shot me a look as we rounded the landing of the stairwell, its stone steps worn smooth and concave with the tread of generations of students.

"Don't call me Jack, nobody calls me Jack." The name, where had it come from? Maybe from all the hours I spent thinking about him, pondering every fact of his existence. I took the rebuke, but happy puppy that I was, only wagged my tail all the harder. Truth was, I was missing him. I had taken to inscribing elaborate scrolls and designs in my notebooks and texts; in places my English survey text looked like an illuminated manuscript. Embedded in these designs, hidden in the scrollwork, were his initials and a motto that kept recurring, "Mo'jo' kelle," which was code for "My own John Kelly." In my feverish imagination I thought this looked like an African word, and since Africa was in the news, no one would suspect. Suspect what? – I didn't own anything.

Judy persisted. In the fall of my junior year – we were both English majors now, determined to become teachers like Burton – I began to encounter her repeatedly in Folwell Hall, where most of the English classes were held. Trudging up the stairs to get to my first class, I'd be surprised to find her standing in the window well on the landing, reading a novel or taking notes, her thoughtful profile framed in soft waves of light brown hair that glinted auburn, backlit by the morning sun. Soon, this sight too became familiar, comforting. Glad to see each other, we'd visit easily. We had so much in common, after all, Burton and school, and as these occasions multiplied, which to my delight they did, we discovered that we had other things in common: a love of jazz, old movies, witty song lyrics from musical comedies, the "sick" comics, the routines of Nichols and May.

It was a seduction of sorts; Judy insinuated her way into my life. Sometimes you don't know how lonely you've been until you're not lonely any more. We began to meet between classes, we studied together at the library, took the same courses, read the same books, wrote papers on the same novels. School was the medium of this friendship but it blossomed forth in countless intimacies, the sharing of stories and feelings about family and friends, expressions of personal longing and disappointment. Soon she was driving me home after school. I had never known such a friend.

Deprived of regular contact, I adopted more desperate measures to see John. I haunted the basement of Shevlin Hall where I knew he sometimes took lunch, racing across campus to pop in at various times during the day, hoping to catch wind of his schedule. On those Friday evenings when I didn't attend the symphony, I sometimes took my dad's car to go to the movies at the nearby Varsity Theater – Bergman, Fellini, Truffaut – hoping to catch him after his concert. On one of those evenings, a slushy winter night, I lucked out and found him standing at a bus stop huddled against the wind; I pulled over and offered him a ride. I learned he was changing his major to journalism; writing was his real passion, he said.

I felt him slipping away. The scraps of information I gleaned from our few encounters only whetted my appetite for more. The stories he told me about his Army buddy roommate, his landlady and her daughter, the guy, practically a stranger, he had wrestled with on the living room floor, tearing his shirt in the process – only made me envious of these people and their proximity to this man, and bitter at my own exile.

By the end of my junior year, Judy and I were best friends. At some point – when does so audacious a thought dare take hold? – I began to feel that she would always be part of my life. I didn't know how, exactly; I simply assumed it. I couldn't imagine my life any other way. Returning to the old loneliness was unthinkable.

Phrases casually crept into our conversation, tag-lines and parentheses that implied a future together: "When we get our PhDs," "When we're teaching," "When we get old, we'll still be figuring it all out." But how to get to this future? I never thought of marriage; I felt no desire for her, no stirrings of tenderness or affection that de-manded a deeper intimacy. We would just always be friends, it was as simple as that. Then the rules changed; they were always changing, just when you were getting comfortable.

Except for occasional encounters, John and I barely saw each other any more. One night, however, I staged a daring coup. I remembered his work schedule – he juggled two part-time jobs – and called the Hotel Leamington to check when his shift as busboy ended. That evening I saw *Never on Sunday* at the State Theater, and as soon as the movie ended, I raced the few blocks to the hotel, arriving breathless and barely able to ask for him, only to learn that he had just left. I tore out of the hotel and sprinted back to Hennepin Avenue where the busses ran, arriving sweaty and exhausted with a sideache, and jumped on the first bus I saw. He might be transferring up ahead. No John. I muttered a feeble excuse to the driver and asked to be let off. I waited for the next bus, which happened to be the one to Robbinsdale. But no John. I decided to stick it out and see if he turned up further down the line. Maybe he'd done an errand after work. My heart sank with each stop – Eighth, Seventh, Sixth, Fifth, Fourth, Third – then suddenly, there he was, mounting the steps with that smile of his. Just as he was about to drop his change into the fare box, I seized his elbow and whisked him off in triumph to my waiting but now distant car.

I sometimes wonder what he must have thought. In my frenzy I probably looked a little like a younger Aschbach in the final pages of Mann's *Death in Venice*, frantic in his furtive pursuit of the beautiful boy Tadzio through the maze of Venetian streets– sans the mascara running down my fevered cheeks. But did John have any more of an inkling of what was happening than I did?

My audacity paid off; I got invited to his house to listen to some records. I tromped the three miles on an unusually warm February afternoon, arriving happily with wet feet in squishy shoes grown warm and cozy with walking. It was a delightful time, free and easy. If I think about it, I can still smell the kitchen, feel the press of carpet on my elbows as we lay beside his portable turntable surrounded by a patchwork of colorful album covers, listening to passages from Verdi's *Requiem* and Berlioz's *Symphonie Fantastique*.

"Is that Sean Berlioz?," I asked.

He laughed. "Why do you say that?"

"Because everybody you like is Irish."

It was getting toward dusk and he walked me part of the way home, with a stopover at the library where we browsed the shelves for awhile.

"I'm amazed at all you know about literature," I said. "You've got a funny or interesting story about practically every title and author. I love hearing you talk."

"Don't flatter me, I don't like it."

"Is it flattery if it's sincere?" Then I spotted a favorite of mine, Thomas Wolfe's *You Can't Go Home Again*. The lush prose intoxicated me. I read a passage about the hero's first impressions of New York street life, then added something I had read in a recent *Atlantic*.

"Wolfe's term for homosexuals was 'twilight people' – shadowy, unreal figures who inhabit the margins of existence."

"Twilight people – that's right. I like that," he said.

Months later I got a return visit to celebrate my getting my own hi-fi system. John brought some of his old records as a gift. Afterwards my mom remarked how handsome he was.

Judy started inviting me over to her house to watch TV in the evenings. We liked the *Dick Van Dyke Show* and *The Defenders* – "Why not watch them together?," she asked. I was reluctant to drive because of my poor night vision but she offered to pick me up and drive me home.

No self-contained heroic gesture here, no neutral setting of library or classroom, no safe, objective medium of books or studies. This was real life, the rec room of her parents' split-level, set off from the rest of the house by a long hall and stairway. Plenty of privacy here, and my Aunt Virginia didn't have to arrange for it either.

The love seat fronted the TV, with just enough room for two, and no matter how carefully I composed myself or how still I sat, we tilted precariously toward one another and my wayward knee kept drifting over. My right arm lay immobile between us like a dead weight, resisting all my efforts to relax and raise it to a more comfortable position on the back of the couch. With each visit that weight grew more leaden, the space between us shrank, and the room, with its low acoustic ceiling, dim lighting and unfamiliar recesses, closed in upon us like one of those compacting rooms in the old Saturday matinee movie serials. When, after several visits, I finally succeeded in raising that arm, getting it to crawl inch by inch up the mountainous terrain of the back of the love-seat, it lay there like a torpid iguana, unable to creep into the warm crevice behind her back. This ground was never gained for good; the ordeal had to be repeated with each visit – the same heroic mustering of will, the same laborious crawl, and at the end, the same ignominious defeat.

Then there was the pound cake, the ritual pound cake that meant the end of the evening, the end of easy conversation about the shows and the looming specter of the long, silent ride home. Pound cake. How appropriate – a pound of flesh. I knew what was expected of me. Nothing was given without something being asked in return. I felt I owed Judy that; she had every right to expect it; it was my duty as a man. Everything pointed to this obligation; it was as if all the forces in the universe had conspired to plant me on this sofa, in this room, beside this woman. Judy, my mother, Burton, my aunt, all the years of social conditioning, the roles and expectations, the bullying and peer pressure, the idealized image of family, the teachings of my church, the middle-class values of my culture, the books I was reading, the whole weight of Western civilization – all pressed down upon me in this space, forcing this test of my mettle and manhood. The failure of that arm, its impotence to creep that extra inch or two, was epic and existential. I didn't belong, I couldn't love, I was a failure as a human being – the nameless fears that had nagged beneath my anxiety as I sat on the couch with Lois in my Aunt Virginia's living room, were here named and owned, and pressurized to a crisis point.

My campaign with John had petered out. I ran into him a few more times on campus, once in Walter Library where he was in a funk about his roommate.

"He's a fruit," he said.

"What are you talking about? You guys are best buddies."

"He's a fruit, and I don't want to talk about it." I don't know what possessed me but I wanted John to meet Burton. The meeting was a disaster; John's only comment afterward was, "He's brilliant, like you said, but what a fairy!"

"You're kidding."

"It's obvious – the way he talks and walks, those gestures with his hands," and he made a flourish with a limp wrist.

While studying at my desk one night, fighting boredom and fatigue, I wondered what it meant for two men to be close to one another. How would they express it? I held this in my mind for awhile, turning it over like an abstract proposition. What would they do? It seemed inconceivable, awkward, even grotesque as I tried to imagine various permutations of limbs and body parts before giving up in disgust. Yet I barely had a better idea of what a man and woman might do, though there at least I had descriptions in books.

Sometime in my senior year, John threw a party at Mrs. Wilson's. I had learned a lot about him; he was much more social than I was, even a party animal, and he liked his sports and liquor too – more of a regular guy all around. I hardly ever went to parties and at this one I did the usual, found a corner and kept to myself. Everyone was drinking too much, especially John, whose loud laughter echoed from every corner of the basement. Mrs. Wilson was kind to me and kept me company as she tended bar. At some point she took John aside and told him I was getting sick and needed a breath of fresh air. I leaned against him as we walked outside, and uttered some inanity about the moon that was meant to be profound before throwing up on his shoes. That's the last I saw of him for awhile.

The evenings at Judy's had become excruciating. For years afterwards I viewed these months as the most horrible period of my life. I decided to see a counselor so I contacted the mental health unit of the Student Health Service.

"I've got a problem," I told the intake nurse over the phone.

"What kind of a problem do you mean?"

"A personal problem – that's why I want to talk to a counselor."

"What kind of a personal problem?"

"Well...uhh... a sexual problem," I said.

"What kind of a sexual problem? We can't help you unless you give us some information."

"I can't talk about it over the phone. I need to see someone." I was assigned to meet with a psychiatric social worker.

While I fidgeted in the waiting room, dwarfed by giant cut-leaf philodendrons, I wrote out my problem on a slip of paper; I couldn't bear to utter the words – I barely knew the words. I had seen a phrase in a recent *Time* magazine article and thought it described my case.

When I entered the office I was relieved to see a woman sitting at the desk. She was sharp-featured, with glasses on a chain that kept sliding down the bridge of her nose, and her dark hair pulled back in a severe bun. I handed her the note.

"I think I may be a latent homosexual. I am becoming very close friends with a woman. She is the most important person in my life and I fear that she expects more from me, a romantic involvement. I don't feel capable. I don't know what to do. I am afraid of losing her."

She looked up at me sharply and said with a note of alarm, "Have you told her yet?"

"No." I was mortified.

"Good, whatever you do, don't. How long have you known this about yourself?"

"Since I was a little kid," and I told her about my dream of my uncle and my history growing up. She seemed as uncomfortable talking about the matter as I was and I was grateful for her reticence.

"Have you ever acted on your feelings?"

"No."

"Good, there's hope for you. You'll be all right."

Then she recommended that I enter one of their therapy groups.

"Will there be other people like me?" I asked.

"Probably not, but it helps to talk your problems out with others, even if they don't have the same issue."

I was appalled. How could she? No way would I talk about this with total strangers; I had never spoken of it before to another living soul. I walked out of the office in despair.

That last evening at Judy's was the worst. I withdrew more deeply into myself. The pound cake sat like lead at the base of my esophagus, the ride home was interminable, the silence suffocating. I knew that if I got out trying to make my escape with the usual pleasantries, the friendship was over. It was over in any case; the tension was unbearable.

In utter hopelessness, feeling that I owed her something, if only the truth, I turned toward her and said, "Judy, I love you but there's something you must know..."

She reached for me and my words trailed off as she said in a tremulous voice, "I didn't know, I wasn't sure." I extended my arms and suddenly the need to finish my statement seemed inconsequential, melting away into a much greater need, to kiss and embrace.

The next day I was exultant. I had joined the human race.

A year later we were married, and although I was beset from time to time by certain longings and attractions, by a gaze exchanged and held too long with a man in a supermarket or parking lot, I told myself that these episodes would soon pass, like bouts of erotic hay-fever in the spring. What mattered was the marriage.

After a year we moved, and one spring day when I was out walking in our new neighborhood, I spotted a man getting out of a red Triumph convertible. It was John. We said hello, I told him I was married, he congratulated me and said he was working in business communication for Prudential. I found out his address, and wrote him a note, most of which is mercifully forgotten, but one phrase sticks out, an apology of sorts, for "forcing my twisted love on you."

It was meant to be magnanimous, delivered from the smug Olympian heights of my marriage; it was also meant to wipe the slate clean. John was history. I had made it.

The Test

I suppose it was a test, that weekend in Madison with my friend Mike, the first time I had been away from my wife in three years of marriage, but then, wasn't everything? Of exactly what, you were never really sure.

I had met Mike two years before in graduate school, where we shared a huge office crammed with too many desks and even more teaching assistants, who squatted in shifts to grade exams and see students. He occupied the desk just behind mine, and our chairs, which rolled too freely for the cramped space, sometimes bumped backs.

"Oops, sorry, there we go again. Hi, my name's Bob Anderson." The acquaintance began easily enough – we were both bookish and loved to talk literature and ideas – but I was surprised to find him soon taking more than casual interest in our comings and goings.

Tall and lean like me, even paler, he had a fine, slightly curly, silken black beard and moustache, and an elegant, almost aristocratic mien. What could he see in me? Bluff and boyish, I was a bull in the china shop of high culture, a mere Scandinavian pretender when compared with this legitimate Jewish intellectual.

It was a grand time, this easy intimacy between us. With a simple clearing of the throat and a "Hey Bob" or a "Hey Mike," a scintillating conversation about Wordsworth and the exhaustibility of memory, or Proust and its inexhaustibility, or Beckett and its irrelevancy, was no more than a squeaky swivel away. Maybe, I speculated, this was merely an accident of propinquity.

I conducted my side of the friendship with my usual reserve, resisting his advances for contact outside of school. Complacent in my new marriage, I responded stingily that summer when his overtures took a plaintive edge. Twice he had asked if my wife and I couldn't include him in our movie plans; his fiancée Nadia was away in Israel visiting her parents. By the following summer, however, after spending many hours together studying for our masters' exams, sharpening our wits on each other, an easy rapport had developed between us. I had a new friend.

I hadn't seen Mike since his move to Madison at the end of that summer to work on a doctorate at the University of Wisconsin, but once I made the decision to visit him the following spring, I could think of little else. The marriage was stagnant. Judy was tired and depressed most of the time, having taken two extra part-time jobs so I could quit teaching and devote myself entirely to my studies, but I was disillusioned with graduate school, feckless and adrift in my life and diddling endlessly with a paper on Shelley… and even more with myself. True to form, we weren't talking about any of this. We slipped past each other wordlessly in the cramped quarters of our apartment. Only years later did I learn she was suicidal at the time.

As the visit approached, my imagination lurched into overdrive. I cruised a parallel universe while some part of me idled back here with Judy. I was dutiful, polite. "Sure, I'll go get the car," but the walk to the dealership, a slow slog through the snow-drifted sidewalks along St. Paul's Marshall Avenue, only provided yet another venue for the real adventure, which was transpiring inside my head. I enacted elaborate scenarios with Mike, trying out quips, bits of dialog and whole conversations. I was in training for my visit, pushing and testing the limits of the friendship. Brilliant and spirited at first, these exchanges often degenerated into bitter quarrels, requiring us to fumble our way back toward making amends. I relished these reconcilements, and occasionally was surprised to find myself in a place of rare sweetness and tenderness, suffused with longing and regret. Hadn't I been here before? I had almost forgotten – the once hallowed, now barely recoverable memory of meeting the boy sitting solitary on the banks of Lake Itasca.

When I got off the bus in Madison, it was like stepping into my dream. Out of the milling crowd, the criss-crossing of countless travelers and their greeters, Mike surfaced with a warm smile and handshake, putting me instantly at ease.

"Here, let me take these." There for a weekend, I had packed enough for a month.

"You'd think I was planning on moving in." I laughed, that cackle that gave him such a kick. I followed his lead as we snaked our way through the jumble of carts, the lines and clusters of people with their piles of parcels and luggage. In the hubbub of the terminal, we quickly found our rhythm and slipped into the old familiar banter, as if our conversation had never ceased.

This was high adventure. I had told my friend Margo that I was taking a "moral holiday." I had no idea what this meant; I wanted to give my trip a tinge of the mock-heroic. But she had chided me playfully anyway, invoking the specter of Burton and a universe governed by implacable moral laws.

Outside in the cool, clear air, the elongated dome of the State Capitol loomed like a watchful bird over the busy commerce below. Mike and I quickly dispatched with small-talk. He told me he was reading the late novels of Henry James and began talking about *The Golden Bowl*.

"Wouldn't it be wonderful to have all that consciousness?," he said. I confessed I found the later novels convoluted and nearly impenetrable.

"James lost it when he started dictating his novels. Some of those sentences run on for pages." I proudly announced I was tackling *Moby Dick* for the second time.

"I'm going to re-read it every decade of my life. It will be my own private River Wye; I'll revisit it periodically just like Wordsworth, as a touchstone to see how far I've come." That got a wry smile from him.

"Don't you think it's weird, Mike, taking something you love, like literature, and making it an object of formal study, like botulism? I just want to teach, that's all. Like Chaucer's clerk – 'Gladly would he learn, and gladly teach.' That's what keeps me going. Why do you put up with all the Mickey Mouse?" I had just about decided to quit graduate school and teach at a community college, which didn't require a Ph.D.

"I'm going to be a poet." Wow, my friend, the poet. Reading, studying and appreciating literature were one thing, but actually writing it, creating it out of your own heart and mind, in the here and now, not dredging it up from some distant, mythic past – I didn't know anyone who was a writer. I was half in awe of him, and half suspicious. How could he presume?

We traded quips and bags back and forth on the two-mile trek to his small rented house in a tidy working-class neighborhood. By the time we got to his door, tired and sweaty, my arms were ready to give out. For as long as I had known him, he had never owned a car. A matter of economics, principle or rebellion? – I couldn't say. Once he had applauded the story of a disgruntled auto worker at the Ford plant in St. Paul who protested working conditions by sealing empty Coke bottles inside the doors of new cars so the mysterious rattling would drive the new owners nuts, discrediting the company. Everyone at the bar had laughed but me; I disapprove.

Inside, the decor was vintage Mike, stripped to essentials. Several pieces of salvaged furniture, a record player and some albums, a couple of Chianti bottles curdled with candle wax, and walls hung with personality posters: Einstein, Freud, D.H. Lawrence, Chaplin, Mae West and Che. Tucked in a corner was a small wrought-iron rack with a clutch of books. Mike, who read more widely and deeply than anyone I knew, borrowed all his books from the library; you couldn't check out a volume with any claim to distinction without seeing his scrawl on the card in the back. He had got there first.

"It's small but it serves," he said. "You'll be sleeping on that roll-away, I sleep on the hide-a-bed by the window. The bathroom's off the kitchen. You can hang your clothes in here," and he opened a small closet just inside the front door. On a hook hung a black flowered oriental robe with the faintest whisper of lavender. He hadn't mentioned Nadia.

I unpacked, washed up and we relaxed at the kitchen table over steaming cups of tea before venturing out to explore the neighborhood. I suggested the alley tour.

"It's not in front yards spruced up for show, but in back yards with their cast-offs and quirky order or disarray, that you get a truer index of how people live, who they really are," I said.

We did a thorough inventory, taking as our purview everything we saw, commenting on matters of taste, class, patterns of urban development and shifting demographics, weaving in stories about our own growing up in WASPish Robbinsdale and the Jewish North Side of Minneapolis. We were brilliant together; it was almost as if we had rehearsed. I know I had. I was in my element, never happier than when I was tagging along with a guy. This proximity in parallel, this easy, rhythmic movement, this patter that was almost physical, palpable – was it more a sense that if I stuck close enough, some of his guyness would rub off on me, or that by some magic of movement I might slip inside his skin?

That evening the day's casual intimacy melted into the more mellow, homely intimacies of sharing a meal and cleaning up afterwards, reading and visiting in neighboring chairs, getting ready for bed and sleeping under the same roof. This was rare, more than I ever could have imagined. I changed into my pajamas in the bathroom but Mike undressed right in front of me, in the living room, peeling off his shirt and undershirt, then his pants and boxer shorts. The glow from the lamp shimmered on the sleek whiteness of his skin, throwing the silken tracery of fine black hair into delicate relief, and when I found my eyes following the furrow like an arrow from chest to belly, then to the dimness unfurling below, I did what I always did in such situations – averted my gaze.

The next day we toured the campus. It was the spring of 1967 and Madison was in ferment. The State House might dominate the prospect of main street, but real political action was spilling out into the streets themselves. Posters and flyers announcing meetings and protests were tacked to telephone poles and trees; graffiti were scrawled on bridge abutments and deserted storefronts: "Stop the War," "Hell, no, I won't go" and "Fuck LBJ." On a plywood construction fence, conscripted for public art and political collage, the word "Amerika" glared, its letters dripping blood, near a Swastika blazoned on a field of red-and-white stripes.

"This is crazy, what's happening," I said.

"No, it's necessary."

"How so?"

"Jefferson believed that the Tree of Liberty had to be refreshed periodically with the blood of tyrants."

"So does Mao. Look at what's happening in Red China with the Cultural Revolution and his gangs of Red Guards."

"Mao got it from Jefferson, who felt that a revolution every nineteen years or so was just the thing to keep the spirit of democracy alive."

"That doesn't make either of them right. Both views are based on an unrealistic notion of human nature, a vision of perfectibility that leads inevitably to totalitarianism."

"Jefferson was a totalitarian?"

"This is not an academic argument, Mike. Besides, who knows what he might have done with a third term, maybe declared everybody yeoman farmers by decree. You ever see those beady eyes of his? – the look of the true believer. I make a point of going to these meetings at the U – the T.A.s are trying to unionize – just to vote against anyone who looks too lean and hungry, too pale and full of zeal. I'm telling you, Mike, these are very scary people."

"Oh Bob, you could be describing yourself." We laughed.

On campus, we stopped at the Student Union to watch a group of young men and women garbed in the colorful cast-offs of street theater, their long hair bound in head scarves and macramé, intent on rushing spring by dancing in the chilly air. The plaza overlooked a leaden Lake Mendota.

Mike lost himself in the scene, finally saying over the blaring rock music, "Look at all that exuberance and animal energy – such freedom!" All I saw were the jerky gyrations of people who seemed remarkably vacant-looking, self-absorbed and unconnected with anything outside themselves.

"They're just expressing urban overcrowding – the alienation and anomie of modern life." My smart re-marks continued as we joined a long line of men at the urinals. "Is this a pee-in?," I asked.

These were intense times, when no remark was neutral, when humor itself was suspect. America was on the verge of its own cultural revolution, polarizing around issues of war and peace, freedom and justice, age, race, class and gender. Parts of cities were going up in flames, the civil rights and student movements were turning violent, and matters as innocent as hair and dress were flash-points dividing families, schools, communities, the nation itself. Nothing was innocent; everything was a statement. Not to speak was to speak, not to act was to act – it was all political. In my own family, Sunday dinners, which had been occasions for free-wheeling, mostly good-natured arguments about politics, religion and philosophy among three generations of Andersons, were turning ugly and divisive. Raised a liberal, having flirted with socialism, I was fast becoming a reactionary in the charged climate of the Sixties. Mike was pulled to the opposite pole; he seemed to revel in the Dionysian energies being unleashed, the prospect of unlimited freedom and possibility. I remembered a simpler time when his favorite honorific in describing someone was "vital"; "spontaneous" ranked a close second.

I sensed a sadness in my friend. Climbing up a hill on the outskirts of the campus, a chore that left both of us breathless, we were quarreling about wars of national liberation, whether they were genuine revolutionary movements or simply tactical skirmishes in the Cold War. Mike invoked Franz Fanon's *The Wretched of the Earth* and a vision of a world fractured by a widening gulf between rich and poor; I cited the high rhetoric of Kennedy's Inaugural, the call to pay any price in the defense of freedom. He grew quiet, and a weariness seemed to settle on him; then he paraphrased Paul's admonition to live in faith, hope and charity – charity being the greatest of these.

"I don't see much *caritas* in the world today, do you?" In the face of his question, all my cleverness evaporated; I had no ready answer for my friend. He was in the throes of his own transformation, as I was in the midst of mine; in a society flying apart and being reconstituted with each convulsion, we were both impelled by forces greater than ourselves, beyond our understanding. There was a ground on which we could not meet.

On our way home, we stopped at a drugstore to check out the magazines. Mike picked up a muscle magazine, something I dared to do only covertly while ducking behind a post or crouching down near the floor, usually in a nervous sweat, breathing rapidly and glancing up every few seconds. He was brazen. He looked at one after another, commenting on the guys' builds, noting one particularly handsome guy's well-developed chest and arms. I couldn't believe it. Was he telling me that he knew about me? – I barely knew about me! Was he teasing me, or revealing himself to me? Was this the way guys, normal guys, were supposed to be, at home enough in their own skins that acknowledging interest in the male body was perfectly natural, a matter of no consequence? Then I definitely wasn't normal. I barely glanced at his pictures, grunting noncommittally while hastily snatching the latest copy of *Harper's* off the rack and burying my embarrassment in a blur of flipping pages.

As we walkked home I wondered, last night when he moved over under the lamp to undress, did he do that intentionally?When we got back to his place, he put on an album, then asked me to step over to the phonograph to listen to a song, "Somethin's Happenin' Here." Afterwards he said, "Listen to those words. Poetry's not dead, but the academic tradition is. The lyric impulse is alive and well in modern rock. It's returned to the popular culture where it was in the Renaissance and before. Early poets were singers too and their work was a vital expression of the culture, not like today when poets are ignored or kept alive only in the Academy."

I knew this was important to him, but it smacked of heresy. Yet I was caught up in the haunting melody and raspy lyrics of the song; with my poor hearing I barely understood the words, but I sensed the mood and heard enough snatches to evoke for me that mysterious, shadowy world at the edge of consciousness that was sometimes prompted by the hungry look in a man's eyes or an attitude struck in a darkened doorway.

What was happening here? Was this a song about my innocence? Had Mike read me in some way I had not been able to fathom myself? Was he hinting at something, inviting it? I perplexed myself with a habit of mind ingrained through years of self-questioning, subjecting every instinct, motive, thought and feeling to test after test... to get at the truth, or get as far away from it as I could. I flashed to the memory of his belly luminous in the lamplight.

"That's a crazy idea! How can you possibly maintain that the poetry of Shakespeare, Wordsworth and Keats is being replaced by Dylan, Joplin and Jagger?" I tore into the argument with relentless energy, which only gradually dissipated in a flurry of academic quarrelling.

Later Mike shared another discovery of his, Galliano. We took our drinks outside and sat on the porch swing, relaxing to its rhythmic squeaking, indifferent to the chilly breeze and gathering clouds, carried along on what seemed an almost endless stream of conversation. Eventually the talk turned to the subject of love. He had just finished Lawrence's *Women in Love* and he talked about passion, the elemental bond between a man and a woman who have chosen each other, the surrender of the personal will to the transpersonal life-force.

I got impatient; this was too theoretical and impractical. But was I missing something? Mike seemed in touch with the deeper currents of life, the complexities of human relationships that always eluded me. He dwelled on the dynamics among the two sets of couples in the novel, emphasizing the homoerotic undercurrent in the bond between the two men, Birkin and Gerald. Was this another clue?

One thing he didn't mention was Nadia, nor had I mentioned Judy. She wasn't on my mind much, but the marriage certainly was; I thought about it often, almost as if it were a third personality independent of Judy and me. I felt fraudulent speaking of love to Mike, only once getting close to what I truly believed:

"It's fine to talk about love, Mike, but I know from my own experience in trying to keep a marriage together, in trying to preserve and honor the commitment you've made to someone, that you have to work hard, damned hard. You have to make sacrifices to preserve the union and the value you place on the beloved. You have to fight against the ebb and flow of time, the corruption of habit and use, the inevitable waning of passion and feeling. I believe that Love is largely a matter of will."

I was eloquent. Knowing little of passion or love, I believed passionately in the idea and institution of marriage. It was central to my identity as a man; insecure in that identity since boyhood, I had learned to pass, had acquired the appropriate attitudes and mannerisms, including finally the most persuasive mannerism of all, marriage.

For the first time Mike and I moved beyond cleverness and academic argument to real, sustained engagement. He took strong exception to my statement. For him love, whether passionate love or friendship, was a supreme value and will had little to do with it. Its medium was the utter candor and reality of two persons who had made themselves vulnerable to one another; its substance, the weaving together of shared moral destinies. Each of us was defending important turf and we sparred until dusk and the air grew cold. The debate unsettled, we went into dinner.

We finished dessert to the rumbling of distant thunder, then repaired to the living room, shared a joint – my first – and knelt beside each other like communicants at the rail, with our elbows over the back of the couch, to watch the gathering storm. He rose to switch off the light, then returned, closer this time. Our knees sank deep into the cushions, tipping us lightly into one another. I felt the warmth of his body, the rise and fall of his breath. We stared intently at the distant flashes, waited a few seconds for the answering report, anticipated the next chorus and lost ourselves in the sequence of diminishing intervals as the storm drew nearer and nearer. Soon the far-off flashes were jagged streaks of light that split the sky with thunderclaps and rattled the windows in their casements.

I had never felt so calm. This was where I belonged. The events of the last day and a half, of the last few weeks and months, of my entire life led inexorably here, beside this man. All the confusion and self-doubt of the last few hours, of a lifetime, lifted in one clarifying moment. I began easily, with words I had never before imagined, much less uttered. They sprang from a source so deep, so pure and clear, they were beyond questioning, perhaps beyond feeling and desire.

"I don't want you to think this is the pot talking, Mike. This is what I really feel, I know it. I want to go to bed with you." A brief silence, then he rose, switched on the light and returned to the couch.

"I don't know, Bob. You've got to understand, with me it's all on the surface."

What did that mean, how could that be? This secret – I had lived with it since childhood, it had been the sweet, shameful focus of my inner life, the piece of grit around which the pearl of my soul had formed. All on the surface? Had I misread Mike and all the signs of the weekend? Was he putting me down? Was he sophisticated in ways I couldn't imagine? Were my feelings inconsequential, the accidental byproduct of a tortured inner life distorted by fantasy? I started to wander in an all-too-familiar maze – the Fun House, I called it. You entered through the clown's gaping, laughing mouth and found yourself bewildered in a hall of mirrors, confronted at every turn of possible action with another image of yourself – tiny or enormous, clear or distorted, in full figure or profile, from the front or rear, or repeated *ad nauseum* in an infinite regress of self-consciousness. You can't get outside yourself, touch anything real; you don't know what you think or feel, who you are, what you want or need. There is no exit, only paralysis.

This time, however, I quickly returned to the clarity of that moment. All barriers fell away between us then and we talked for hours. He asked if I had ever been sexual with a man and I said no but that I had known about myself since age five. I told him everything: the loneliness, the sense of freakishness, how Judy had drawn me out of my shell and how I had come to love her despite myself.

"I've always been attracted to women," he said, adding that he had experimented with boys a couple of times in junior high and had experienced occasional feelings of attraction toward men. Then he told me that he and Nadia had broken off their engagement, speaking with anguish about last summer. "It was a hell of lust – do you know what I mean?"

What did I know of love or lust? Lust was mainly an abstraction I associated with medieval homiletic literature. Married three years, in some sense I was a virgin still, innocent of the world of desire. Innocence was my persona, my defense against an array of forces that threatened my very integrity, my identity as a human being. I barely understood, much less connected with his stories of sexual obsession.

"Since moving to Madison I've met a woman from Chicago and I think I'm falling in love with her," he said. "I don't understand it. Susan has short, stubby legs; I'm always attracted to women with long, graceful legs. Nadia had beautiful legs." He looked at me as if I would have noticed.

"Ah, it's HER robe in the front closet," I said. Many pieces from the weekend were starting to fall into place. Mike told me all about Susan, leaned back languorously in his chair, sighed and stretched his full length, closed his eyes and said, "I wish she were here right now – I feel such desire for her."

I too closed my eyes and began to hallucinate under the influence of the pipe we were passing back and forth. A tender image of a young girl surfaced, perhaps eight or nine years old, sitting on the stoop of my family's cabin on North Star lake. She was surrounded by tall, sinuous paper-white birches that thrust their shimmering waxy green leaves high into an electric blue sky. Her face was averted but I knew it was Judy. Then I saw a black-

and-white snapshot of my grandma dressed in her Sunday best that I had taken as a kid at the State Fair with my Brownie Hawkeye. The wrinkles in her face began to dance as she mugged for the camera, while all my relatives milled and mugged in the background; with each successive frame of memory she grew younger and younger until she merged indistinguishably with photos we had taken of Judy mugging in an airport photo booth. The frames of Judy flashed rapidly until she was like an animated cartoon figure doing a jerky strobe-lit Charleston while her hair grew long and snaked its way down and around her jubilant, wildly gyrating body.

Was this love, I wondered, this dissolving force that radiated from a single act, a kernel of pure freedom, to break down all barriers, even time itself, uniting everything in delight? Under its generous influence I had been given Mike, my wife, my grandmother and my whole family fresh, anew. I had never loved so much.

I shared all of this and more with Mike, and he responded in kind as we talked late into the night. I had never known such closeness.

"I worried that we couldn't be friends, not true friends, after your remark about love and will," he said. "But I know now that we will always be friends."

When it came time to go to bed, Mike went into the kitchen to clean up while I got the roll-away ready and undressed. I was getting under the covers when he came out. He sprawled on the couch across the room from me, threw his head back, then looked at me, drained, distraught.

"I could go to bed with you, Bob, but you have to understand, it would be lust, only lust, you have to understand that."

"I'm O.K., Mike." I was supremely happy; I didn't need one other thing from him. I pulled the covers over my shoulders, tucked them tightly under my chin and fell easily asleep.

"And slept the sleep of the just," I am tempted to write. There's a part of me still, after all these years, that wants to judge this young man, to see his gesture as complacent and evasive, preserving intact the protective pose of the *pure*. In the years to come, he would pay for this. But his bravery and purity of heart move me. From this distance I cannot touch him, the mystery of his soul. If that weekend in Madison was a test – and wasn't everything? – what exactly was being tested, and did he pass or fail?

Return

Watching the rolling hills of the Wisconsin land-scape sail past, I was giddy on the bus ride home, as if a great weight had suddenly lifted. I felt alive and at home in my own skin, as I imagined Mike and other people, real people, must feel. I wanted to stomp and shout, laugh and cry, tell everybody what had happened.

But what, exactly, had happened? The gravity of my situation quickly reasserted itself when Judy picked me up at the terminal. She was nervous and tense, not unusual for her, but also distant, avoiding almost all eye contact. I asked how the visit with her parents had gone that weekend and got the familiar litany of complaints delivered in that self-checking staccato monotone of hers, which triggered the usual response in me, impatience masked by sympathetic murmurings. She asked perfunc-tory questions about my weekend, and I responded in kind. If she noticed anything, she didn't say.

The next day, however, my friend Marhgo no-ticed, and began probing with her usual lack of tact. "C'mon, Bob, what's goin' on with you? You're high as a kite – I've never seen you this way."

"Nothing, I just had a really great time, that's all."

"Yeah, but what happened? You act like somebody who just got laid."

"Jeez, keep it down, will you?" I glanced nervously at the Students studying nearby. "Mike and I just got really close." I gave her a sanitized version of the weekend, minus the proposition. "I've never felt so close to a guy – it was terrific."

"Yeah, sure. Did you go to bed? Did you screw? That's great. I want all the details."

"God, I can't tell you anything!," I hissed, leaning across the table. "You've got the crudest imagination." She chortled, I giggled and under her wicked tutelage spilled the whole story.

Two nights later, after much thought, I told Judy. We were lying in bed playing our usual game of footsie to see if I was interested enough to initiate love-making. The hush in the room was palpable. I was stalling, mustering the nerve to complete the sentence I had begun the night we first declared our love for one another. "Something happened in Madison," I began, and she said she wondered. "Mike and I got really close," and I told her what had happened, including my fears about myself. She was quiet. A car gunned in the distance, then its lights flickered across the ragged shades, briefly illuminating a room rimmed with boxes and bags, stacks of papers and books teetering against each other.

"I wouldn't worry about it, Bob. I sometimes feel attracted to women too." We lay next to each other silently; we didn't make love that night, nor for many weeks afterwards. Her comment was meant to be reassuring, I suppose, and I should have felt relief that the matter was out in the open at last with so little consequence, but instead I felt empty and numb.

Then I did one of my famous disappearing acts. I could be with Judy and not with her, watching myself go through the motions. While she busied herself around our small apartment, I lay for hours on the couch, the bed or sometimes the living room floor, where she had to step carefully around my six-foot two-inch frame.

> *... In the room the women come and go*
> *Talking of Michelangelo...*

Snatches from T.S. Eliot's "The Love Song of J. Alfred Prufrock" floated in and out of my mind. My theme song – from the first time I had read it, I had adopted it as a mocking gloss on the futility of my existence. In these states I was neither asleep nor awake, my eyes could be open or closed, my breathing was shallow and forced, almost willed. I was absolutely immobile, like a mummy under glass. "Premature rigor mortis," I sometimes called it. I was watching myself intently, studying this peculiar specimen under glass.

> *And when I am formulated – sprawling on a pin,*
> *When I am pinned and wriggling on the wall...*

"Is anything the matter?," Judy asked.
"No."
"Are you sure?"
"I'm fine. Just thinking."
"Will you help me with this?"
"You bet." I got up to take a box down from the hall closet. At least my height was good for something– certainly more useful vertically than horizontally.

"We need to take these over to my parents tomorrow. Will you come with me? I want to ask Dad for some money. We're running short."

"Sure." I resumed the position. This went on for days. I performed all essential functions – ate, eliminated, attended class, studied, communicated when necessary. Mainly, however, I lay and watched myself.

The reality of my situation – the full weight of the marriage and all its responsibilities, the commitment I had made to Judy, the considerable investment in the future, family, moral legitimacy and social acceptance that marriage represented – all pressed down upon me. Beside these concerns, my mere personal predicament looked puny indeed. What were my frustrated longings anyway, these vague, unimaginable yearnings, but another name, a more sordid name to be sure, for the restlessness that afflicts all humanity, that must be conquered at all costs if anything worthwhile is to be achieved? And what did Mike count for in the grand scheme of things? To be perfectly frank, did I even care for him anyway, or was he simply the random target of this restlessness? I rehashed and second-guessed everything that happened that weekend.

> *... It is impossible to say just what I mean!*
> *But as if a magic lantern threw the nerves in*
> *patterns on a screen...*

During this period Judy and I sketched each other, sitting in opposite chairs. My drawing of her, which I have to this day, is precise, meticulous; in those days when I had much more vision, I was a very good draftsman. She's recognizable, though there's a grim set

to her mouth, a severe cut to her bangs. You could manu-
facture her blouse from the details in the drawing: the
tight pleats around the square yoke at her neck, the
French cuffs, the fullness and folds of her sleeves, the
double darts at her chest. Her drawing of me was rough,
its lines tentative and sketchy – she was not a trained art-
ist – but it had a certain quality, sensitive, tender, evoca-
tive... even sexy. The boyishly handsome young man sitting so earnestly at his task touched me. I wish I had it
still; I might be able to capture him better, as he was then.

I started to compose a letter to Mike in my head,
and as it took shape I gradually pulled out of my depression. Its tone I remember well: severe, unflinching honesty. I subjected my behavior, my statements, my feelings
and motivation, all the events of that weekend, to the
most rigorous moral scrutiny. Burton would have been
proud of me. I remember only one phrase; I disparaged
my visit as a "moral holiday."

For a long time I didn't hear back from Mike.
Then one day about four months later, walking across the
Washington Avenue bridge, I met Larry, a mutual friend,
who told me Mike had married recently, a woman from
Chicago, he thought.

Mike's letter arrived weeks later. He too had
taken a long time to write, he said, but for different reasons. He challenged again my notion that love was
largely a matter of will.

"The question is not really theoretical," he wrote.
"The heart of the matter is two people, what they expect
of one another, and what, beneath expectation, excuses
the effrontery of expectation." He accused me of a lack of
good faith: "Do you or do you not want to talk about
what happened? I feel at times as if I were in the presence

of Jehovah in the guise of J. Alfred Prufrock who wonders after the Creation, 'And I see that it might not be good, perhaps.'" I was furious.

Months later when Mike and Susan were in town, Larry hosted a dinner for some friends to which Judy and I were invited. Nothing was said about the weekend or the letters, and Mike invited us to visit them in Madison, which we did that summer. It was a strange visit. Judy didn't say much and stayed in the background. She wore dark glasses, even at the dinner table. An allergic reaction, she said – light hurt her eyes. Mike and I sparred continually. After one tedious four-hour argument about the legitimacy of violent political protest, from which we were rescued only by the call to dinner, Mike awkwardly extended his hand. "Still friends, O.K.?" I thought the gesture odd but shook anyway. When we left the next morning, he handed me a bound copy of the sonnet sequence he had been working on for the past two years. He said the last poem – it had a section all to itself – was about my visit the previous spring. He was busy working on his current project, an epic poem about Leon Trotsky.

That's the last I saw of him. Occasionally I'd run into Larry on campus and he'd tell me some recent news: Mike had moved with Susan to Ireland where he could live cheaply enough to devote more of his time to writing.... Mike and Susan had born a son and moved to Paris.... Mike had run off with a long-legged nightclub dancer from Haiti and moved to the Caribbean... Then nobody heard from him, not Larry, not his brothers, not even his mother and father. He disowned and severed all ties with his family and country of origin. Rumor had it that he had changed his name and was working as a free-lance correspondent covering Haitian politics.

Three times over ten years – each time I rewrote this story, struggling to get it right – I tried to locate him; I called his mother twice, tracked down Larry in France, located his younger brother in Manhattan, all to no avail. I can't recover him or that weekend any more than I can recover any part of myself or my past; like the present, they slip through my fingers like a rushing stream. What is this compulsion to retrieve the past? A friend who recently turned seventy says the past gets more vivid and tangible with every passing year; sometimes he feels he can almost reach out and touch it. Is this yearning a function of age and awareness of mortality, a desire to live more fully what slipped through your fingers the first time... or a need to understand and make whole?

Arabesque

The owlish young man mounts the bus steps vacantly, banging his oversized briefcase against the metal stairwell. He pays, takes his transfer with a mumbled "thank you" and wanders, muffled in winter clothes, to his customary seat by the rear door. Along the way his downcast eyes glimpse folded hands, a knee jutting into the aisle, a flash of red somewhere among shadowy, sleeping forms, a face buried in folds of newspaper – but mostly the narrow, safe stretch of rubber flooring tracing in its damp corrugations the way to his habitual spot.

His seat receives him as usual. He settles, leaving a space between himself and the form by the window. He glances expectantly at the bus signs, hoping to receive from them acknowledgement of his comfortable arrival. He looks down the row of heads he now belongs to, aligns himself slightly, and meditates on the precision of perspective that regularizes diverse humanity.

It is difficult to say when he first notices it – the pressure on his knee. Has his leg relaxed, drifted over? There it is: a faint, dull pressure, almost imperceptible but increasingly persistent the more he thinks about it.

He adjusts his knee, poises himself more precisely near the edge of the seat and resumes his reflections. Before long – it is difficult to say just how long – he notices it again, that comfortable repose of his respectful knee. It can't be him this time. Then he recalls the old Shelley Berman routine about two lovers holding hands at the movies: who's to say whose hand is sweaty? He adjusts his knee again and balances it neatly in front of him. Ever so gradually the sense of repose returns, and after a time he feels a slight modulation of pressure, almost a faint pulsation.

No, he must be imagining it. The pulsation returns – the jacket of the man next to him must be rubbing his leg. The pressure increases; the motions, at first tentative, become regular – it can't be the man's jacket. Some accident must be happening; the man must be absent-mindedly moving his fingers and unknowingly brushing against the leg. Again he moves, and again – delicately, tentatively – the motions resume. He looks even more intently ahead, glancing at the signs for some reassurance. His whole being, immobile, intent, focuses on his leg, but his eyes remain fixed ahead, as if afraid of what they might see. The motions increase in intensity, regularity... persistence. They seem to move more freely over his leg now, not just on the side but on the knee, yet so gently they hardly seem threatening or strange.

He senses the form, warmth, weight and smell of the man beside him, whose presence is summed up in... that finger, that delicate finger – he glimpses it now!, almost involuntarily with the corner of his being – that tiny finger tracing fragile arabesques on heavy tweed. He poises more perilously on the edge of his seat, again reins in his vision, all powers committed to maintaining balance. He wants to leave, but stays, renouncing the stranger with immobile face and unresponsive knee.

When his transfer stop comes, he's relieved to gain a graceful exit. Outside, in the brisk air, perched on brittle snow in the deepening dusk, it strikes him that his leg aches.

* * * *

He puts the transfer in the extended hand and walks to his usual seat. Settled, he prepares for the home stretch. He looks to the ads and then at his row, but it is curiously deserted; people are scattered throughout the bus. He attempts to fix his gaze but his eyes wander, imperceptibly at first, soon tracing objects at the outskirts of vision. He tries to exhume the face from the folds of the evening paper, the patch of red from the recesses of memory.

He looks to the rows of metal supports, then at the line of lights leading in neat perspective toward wife and home, but his eyes wander. They sketch the profile of a young girl and withdraw; they trace the fingers of an old man's hand and follow the bony contours along arthritic joints; they note the shiny heads of children, and linger on the down of a boy's neck, following the tawny furrow into the dimness of the collar. They retreat and begin again their halting search. They hunt the edges of vision, the shadowy places, tracing delicate arabesques among random, anonymous figures.

I wrote this in a white heat when I was twenty-eight and teaching at Minneapolis Community College, two years after my visit to Mike. It is part of the historical record, an account of me as I was then, not as I remember myself. It was cathartic; I had to write it – it practically

125

wrote itself. I came home from that bus ride excited, disturbed and probably aroused, though I couldn't admit that to myself. The insistent fact of that finger pressing in upon all my defenses threatened to implode the entire structure of denial.

When I finished the piece, I felt immense relief. I showed it to Judy when she got home from shopping; then shared it as soon as I could with my mother, father, brother and sister-in-law. It was the first creative writing I had ever done, but more to the point, it was a confession of sorts. "Look, this is who I am – really am," I remember thinking as I handed it excitedly to each person. This weird reclusive figure, so passive, so much in control, so out of touch with himself and his feelings – "This is really me, don't you see?" And even though I was concealing as much as confessing the truth – the story is riddled with literary artifice– I wanted them to grasp the underlying premise: the frustration, repressed desire and hidden identity of the narrator. "Don't you see? Look harder."

Yet why should they acknowledge what I was not ready to admit myself? I had veered close to confession, but not quite, and in any case confessing is not the same as owning. Mike had said as much when he chided me for the self-critical tone of my letter to him, excusing his severity by saying, "The dialectical opposite of confession is chastisement." I resented that statement then, and only now understand it. He lamented as a friend my lack of self-acceptance, my shrinking back, but I couldn't hear the hurt beneath his words. So why should my family hear the hurt beneath mine? They had as much invested in the structure of denial as I did. My owning my identity would overturn their world as much as mine.

Doppelganger

When the nurse brought my daughter out of the delivery room, red and wizened from birth, cupping her chin so I could get a good look at her face, I felt a shock of recognition. It was as if I had known her forever! Yet the curious dance we did as she grew up was a dance of attraction and repulsion.

Rachel was a tomboy, a beautiful little girl with a tawny complexion that positively glowed in pink, who would have nothing to do with dressing up, not even to please her grandmothers on their birthdays. In her regulation outfit of jeans, t-shirt and tennies, her sun-bleached page-boy plastered slick against her forehead, she played as hard and rough as any boy in the neighborhood.

On her eighth Christmas Judy's parents gave Rachel a policeman's uniform, complete with light blue shirt, navy pants, cap, badge, gun, holster, handcuffs and nightstick. Whenever Rachel donned her costume, she was transformed. She looked fierce, puffed out her chest and swaggered as she swung her arms from side to side. Lining up the neighbor kids in the driveway, she'd pace back and forth in front of them, barking orders, leaning into their faces as she interrogated them before snapping on the handcuffs and hauling one of them into custody. Rachel loved this uniform; Judy and I came to hate it.

"You don't have to be brutal," I scolded after one of these episodes. "Kids don't like to be bossed – would you? Besides, policemen can be nice and respectful – why don't you try that sometime? And you know what, things are changing. Women are police officers too. Why don't you play a policewoman once in awhile? – I bet they'd do things differently."

She only glowered at me and stomped off to the sanctuary of her room. As usual, I had droned on too long, lecturing and badgering her. Maybe her caricatures of authority were hitting too close to home. Once before, in a different context, she had responded to my pontification playfully by reaching for my Adam's Apple and twisting with her fingers as if turning down the volume on the TV. It had cracked us up.

We were very close. We could kid and joke about almost anything, I could play every bit as hard as she could, and we were confidants, able to share our innermost thoughts and feelings easily, without defensiveness. But this affinity had a shadow side. As if each of us were the projection of the other, we scrutinized each other, monitoring every mis-step and deviation from the norm.

When I was a little boy, my maiden Aunt Augusta, a devout Missouri Synod Lutheran, used to send me cartoons in the mail clipped from the latest *Ladies' Home Journal*. These panels depicted a child caught red-handed in the midst of some misdeed, thinking he could get away with it, while an ugly bird with stick legs, a black fan tail and an incredulous stare in its goggle eyes spied on the miscreant from around a corner, over a wall or behind a bush. The caption read, "This is a Watchbird watching you." I was Rachel's Watchbird, she was mine.

I felt my very nature was the issue for her – who I was, what I valued, what I thought set me apart from the common herd. Having grown up a sissy, thinking myself an outcast, I had invented my own private notion of masculinity. I would be different from the ordinary guy – sensitive, aware, reflective, cultured, a champion of women and everything they stood for... and a critic of my own sex. I would fit in on my own terms.

Rachel would have none of it. Because I loved opera, dance, classical music, books, poetry and big, luscious words, she loathed them. She groaned when I played Bach on the stereo, galumphed oafishly when I watched ballet, and rolled her eyes and wrinkled her nose whenever I used words like "scrumptious" or "delectable" at the dinner table. This went beyond the usual child's rejection of the parent.

I had a habit in church when listening intently, of leaning forward in the pew with my elbows resting on my knees and my chin cupped in my upturned palms. One Sunday Rachel whispered to me, "Dad, don't do that."

"Why?"

"It looks weird – people might think you're gay."

"That's nuts," I said. These ridiculous tell-tale signs that people were always concocting to decipher if someone was gay or not. Why did they care, what difference did it make? Nevertheless, for several weeks thereafter I sat up straighter in the pew.

The uniform became a flashpoint between us. I was obsessed, and that obsession deepened her defiance. I tried a series of measures: I distracted her, suggesting other activities like playing with her gerbils; I rationed its use; I even hid the damn thing, hoping she'd forget about it. All to no avail, however. She read in it, cleaned her room in it and marched around the house swinging her nightstick like a soldier in an army of occupation. I was beside myself.

Weeks passed until one night when we were driving home from Judy's parents. The silence in the car was broken when Rachel started crying in the back seat.

I reached round to comfort her. "What's wrong, Hon?"

Through the sniffles she sputtered, "I think I need to see a psychiatrist." Where on earth did she get these ideas?

"Why do you say that?"

She couldn't stop crying, but with some gentle coaching, she finally blurted it out: "I think I might be gay."

Damn TV, I thought, putting ideas like that in her head. Kids these days had to grow up way too fast – too much information, too many issues thrust in their faces, too much pressure. It was lots easier in my day; kids could be kids. They were entitled to their innocence.

"Honey, you don't have to worry about things like that now – it's way too early. You've got a whole lifetime ahead of you to figure things out, like who you're attracted to, who you're going to fall in love with. You don't need to label yourself now. You have lots of feelings inside you, feelings for boys, feelings for girls, and you'll have lots more as you get older. You'll have plenty of time to sort it all out."

But she was inconsolable. "Why do you think you might be gay?"

"Because of the way I feel about girls."

"But you like boys too," I countered. It was the age of the Hunk on TV, and Rachel had an eye for a good-looking guy, a great bod and a sexy smile – Tom Selleck was a favorite. Whenever she called me over to look, I was studiously nonchalant, careful not to stare. I re-minded her, "You're always saying how cute the guys are on TV."

"But guys are cute the way puppies are cute," and she wailed. That was my Rachel – a truth-teller who al-ways cut to the chase. I was floored and left defenseless.

"O.K., Honey, we'll get you in to see a psychia-trist. They'll help you; it'll be all right."

When Judy pulled up to the house, Rachel got out and went to her room. Standing in the driveway I turned to Judy, who as usual had managed to stay out of the fray; she didn't like conflict.

"It's so hard, I didn't know what to say," I said.

"You did just fine, Bob." I reached for her and be-gan to sob from somewhere deep inside, heaving against her. She stiffened and pulled away. "Don't."

For years I had watched Rachel play out her sexuality with a remarkable aplomb, so innocent, un-complicated and all on the surface. I watched from the sidelines at a comfortable remove, with fascination and amazement. Somewhere deep in the back of my mind the thought would flicker, Had I been like this once, was she playing out my story too? These thoughts barely had a chance to surface, however, cross-checked by ingrained habits of denial. If I wasn't gay, then neither was she; if my same-sex feelings were inconsequential, then so were hers. So I watched her play out her little drama, which was both her story and mine, with a certain detachment and lack of empathy, a numb wonder.

I had watched Rachel sit in front of the TV at age three or four and start to rock whenever a flashy blonde appeared – the flashier, the better – crooning to herself repeatedly, "She's my honey, she's my honey." Sometimes she leaned forward to plant a peck on the screen. I watched the peculiar adventures with Mrs. Beasley, a cute rag-doll with grandmotherly spectacles and a pull cord in the back that made her talk. Rachel's intimacies with this doll were sacrosanct, always conducted behind closed doors and attended with great embarrassment should either Judy or I chance to intrude. She got flustered whenever I teased her about what went on behind those doors. Later, I listened as she confessed to me her fear that she liked playing nurse with Lisa, the girl next door, too much and was afraid it was becoming a bad habit she couldn't break. Then there was the afternoon she had come home after tearing around the neighborhood with a pack of boys, including Lisa's older brother Billy, whom she admired inordinately. She ran to her room, threw herself on the bed and between sobs began screaming, "I wish I was a boy, I wish I was a boy." As I sat beside her on the bed, my hand resting lightly on her heaving back, what could I say?

I had in my own childhood a perfect analog for nearly everything in hers, including the fascination with cross-dressing, but I could barely remember the boy who stole downstairs, took his mother's red-plaid ruffled curtains from the old metal trunk, stripped off his t-shirt and wound the musty fabric around his body before twirling almost to dizziness in the magical half-light of the basement. I didn't want to remember him. That boy was gone, banished, so thoroughly subsumed in the man triumphantly detached from all that he had ever been, that as I watched my daughter with that strange fascination, I could barely understand, much less connect with the child that she was, the boy I had been. If she was a strange visitor from another world, that world was childhood, and it was lost to me forever.

I made arrangements for Rachel to go to the Washburn Child Guidance Clinic in Minneapolis, and a few weeks later we met as a family with her counselor. Moira was young, attractive, intelligent, articulate, poised and totally in command, with just the right touch – the perfect female role model to help Rachel feel comfortable in her own skin, I thought. Moira explained that she would test and assess Rachel, and counsel her individually; Rachel would interact with a peer group and participate in activities designed to modify behavior through a system of assigning points and rewards. She would act as a mediator between Rachel and us, and work with Judy and me to build effective parenting skills.

Rachel needed a mediator? We weren't good enough parents? She was a co-equal branch of family government? Come on, this was going too far – definitely more than I had bargained for. Then I remembered her crying in the back seat, and why we had come. Besides, Moira was so competent, and we felt so helpless. The issue was far more than the uniform and confusion about sexual orientation. Judy's passivity, my aggressiveness, and Rachel's getting caught in the middle, playing each of us against the other, all contributed to unclear expectations, inconsistent behavior, poor communication and a breakdown in family dynamics. We were a case-study in dysfunction.

Moira was an effective advocate. In her first session with Judy and me, after an initial assessment and meeting with Rachel, she didn't mince words: "Don't make a big deal about the uniform. She doesn't like it when you interfere with her play. That's the main message that comes across. Take the pressure off the whole issue of sexual identity and orientation. Relax. Don't try to make her wear dresses to please her grandmothers on their birthdays. Just take the pressure off; defuse the whole issue, let it lie dormant, work itself out. And don't butt into her playtime – it's sacred."

Chastened, we listened. It was good to hear Rachel's voice given credence through Moira's authority. Rachel gained confidence knowing she had such a powerful advocate, knowing that we paid attention. Through Moira's counseling with us, we learned how to listen, negotiate and manage conflict more effectively; and over the weeks and months, as Rachel gained in self-esteem through better interpersonal skills from the behavior-modification program, family life became easier. We worked together as a team in a spirit of mutual cooperation. Nothing more was said about the uniform, wearing dresses or Mrs. Beasley, and it all went away, became moot, the entire issue of sexual orientation, as if it had never arisen in the first place.

I felt so comfortable with Moira, so trusting of her practical wisdom, that in one of Judy's and my last sessions with her, I alluded to my own issues with sexual orientation, giving her a brief primer on my history. I wondered if she could help me make sense of it, see how it fit into my life.

"Have you ever acted on your feelings?," she asked.

"No."

"How old are you – 36, 37? If you haven't acted on it by now... I don't believe you're gay." As simple as that, she dismissed it, and as always, when someone reassured me, especially someone as authoritative as Moira, I took it too readily to heart, convinced myself all over again and lost the courage of my questioning.

Like clockwork, Rachel's sexuality went underground. She was eight years old, the age when children typically enter the period of latency, according to Freudian psychology. Hers went underground... while mine started bubbling slowly to the surface.

HOME FREE

The Formula

My time at Llewellyn Publications – the Witch Factory, as some of us called it – had been a turning-point. I came into my own vocationally, felt good about myself for the first time in my life, and my gay feelings came roaring to the fore.

I had never felt comfortable as a teacher. I left sweat marks on the blackboard – I backed up against it as if recoiling from my students – because of anxiety in the classroom. It seemed that no matter how dedicated I was or how carefully I had prepared, as soon as I began speaking, my words turned to gibberish and I lost all conviction; I faltered in a tangle of explanation and justification, as if suddenly forced to defend myself against a crowd of silent accusers. I could almost hear them whispering, "You are a fraud, you are false, your life is a joke, you know nothing of real life, you have nothing of value to offer us, why don't you just crawl into a hole and die." This only made me pump the words into the void all the more stridently.

Why was so much of my life about justification? Years later, after I had come out and begun to make peace with myself, I visited a Tarot reader, a delightfully quirky woman who padded about her cluttered house in large fluffy slippers and a quilted housecoat, followed by a haze of cigarette smoke and a retinue of pampered cats. Madame Shirley sat down at a table, brushed aside one of her purring familiars, and began slapping down the cards one after another.

"Numerologically speaking, you're a seven. You're highly intuitive but you mistrust your intuitions." The story of my life, I thought – maybe there was more to that Llewellyn mumbo-jumbo than I thought. She studied the cards for a minute, then said, "I've got to say this, you're lazy." Ouch. She continued as if she had known me for years: "You spend way too much time justifying and explaining yourself. It undermines your credibility with people, who would otherwise be inclined to follow you because of your natural gifts." Old habits die hard, I thought to myself.

At Llewellyn, I had found a job that fit my talents and temperament like a glove. I was a natural in publishing; I loved words and language, felt at home with books and ideas, and I relished the production process, every phase of it, from the glamour of working with authors and manuscripts to the grunt-work of proofreading and keeping deadlines. And I surprised myself, I was good at it. I felt a surge of mastery and confidence, accompanied by a rush of expansiveness; I reached out to people, befriended and counseled them, and they in turn were drawn to me. My small office, tucked in the attic of an old mansion on St. Paul's Summit Avenue, became a gathering place for one and all. Almost forgotten was the freakish, reclusive figure of my twenties, a man who would go to almost any lengths to avoid colleagues and acquaintances, once trapping himself in the "Fire Escape Only" stair-shaft of the university library to dodge his office-mates who were happily visiting in the main stairwell. This new man embraced life, took to heart the words of the Barbra Streisand song that had previously mystified him: "People, people who need people, are the luckiest people." I was a lucky man.

But an odd thing happened. My gay feelings, usually repressed and comfortably stashed in the back-ground, with only occasional flare-ups, came raging to the surface and would not be denied. I was turning my head at every handsome man I passed on the street, fantasizing about some of the guys who were morning regulars on my bus, and I had developed a reckless crush on the maintenance man at Llewellyn who doubled as mail-order astrologer. One morning I went so far as to arrive early to write a mash note, which I wisely tore up before laying it on his desk. I was in a fever.

It wasn't supposed to be this way. I had bought into a contrary theory, that my gay feelings were bound up with depression and low self-esteem. I got this explanation from a therapist I had seen several years earlier regarding a crush on a male student of mine which was making me miserable.

"Would you say you feel more depressed when your homosexual feelings are most prominent?," he asked me.

"Yes."

"Don't you see, there's a connection. Avoid homo-sexual associations and thoughts, and you probably won't feel so depressed; and if you keep yourself positive and upbeat, the homosexual feelings won't be so strong."

I seized on his formula, greedy for another pretext to renounce my treasonous nature.

This was 1968, before Stonewall, before gay rights, before homosexuality was expunged from the official list of psychiatric disorders. The University of Minnesota Psychology Department had recently been testing the effectiveness of aversion therapy with homosexual men by hooking volunteers up to electrodes and administering shocks of varying intensity whenever the subjects responded with arousal to erotic photographs of men.

Dr. Thompson, a member of that faculty, was on the verge of retirement and not taking any new clients, but he said I was bright and there was hope for me because I had never acted on my desires, so he gave me a one-session crash course in homosexual prevention.

"The first thing you need to do is get out of English – too many homosexuals." Then he gave me a quick thumbnail sketch of my affliction – "You won't find this in any textbook, it's my own synthesis" – something about my personality being arrested in an infantile narcissistic stage of development. He told me to stand up straighter – "You look like a whipped dog." And as we left the office, he gave me a friendly pat on the rear, I suppose just to show me I was one of the guys. I was cured.

I didn't leave English, not then and not for that reason, but I did adopt his formula. It held a morbid comfort for me. Its self-contained circularity, admitting of no other reality, perfectly suited my single-minded determination to deny my nature. Good student that I was – I had been given a lesson, hadn't I? – I worked hard to maintain a positive attitude and sure enough, eventually the depression lifted and my homosexual feelings abated. The formula worked.

142

Until Llewellyn, that is. There I discovered a different equation, that my homosexual feelings were linked not with depression and low self-esteem, but the exact opposite. As entrenched as I was in denial, not even I could discount the evidence of my senses: I felt good about myself, I was happy, exultant, and feeling terrifically gay.

This required another look, so I went to a second therapist, two and a half sessions this time – Bruce was leaving counseling for radiology. It was 1975, I was thirty-four, the father of a four-year-old, and my purpose had changed; I wasn't seeking to get rid of my gay feelings, but only to understand them better, see how they fit into my history and personality. I was still committed to my marriage, and I have to confess, that's often how I thought of it, not so much in personal terms, committed to Judy and Rachel – though I loved them deeply – but committed to marriage itself, the idea, the institution, the grand and sacred project passed down from generation to generation, that embodied the highest ideals of civilized social order. It had to be big, because it was standing in contravention of something even bigger – dare I say, the holiness of the heart's affections?

Without appearing, perhaps not even intending to judge, Bruce handed me two deadly tools with which I could begin to dismantle the stirrings of insight I was gaining from my experience at Llewellyn. I told him about my crushes on men, feeling almost overwhelmed by my inability to verbalize them; they were so powerful, romantic and impossibly sweet.

"What makes you think your lust is any different from anybody else's? We all have to struggle with it."

Lust. In all my tight-assed moralism I had never

thought of my feelings that way. Looking back, I wonder how much of a sexual component my longing actually had; part of denial was a determined innocence. And yet I believe there was something genuinely innocent about my feelings. Lust. This made a kind of sense; at least it rejoined me with the rest of humanity, and it appealed to my conservatism. Fighting lust – what better way to man the ramparts of the West?

The second tool was equally deadly. I was ready to begin looking at the subject of homosexuality for the first time in my life, and Bruce suggested I do some reading. Avid reader that I was, I had shied away from books on the subject, just as I avoided Hennepin Avenue because it was rumored that homosexuals haunted some of its bars and bathhouses. The structure of denial was a monolith; it had been built brick by brick, year by year, from childhood through adolescence to adulthood, built at untold cost and sacrifice, the mortar compounded of my life's blood, the integrity of the whole depending on the implacable fit of every single part. I thought I was ready to begin looking at the subject, but books were absolutely the wrong approach.

By default, I lapsed into scholarly, critical mode. With analytical skills honed by years of academic training, I dissected and demolished the explicit and implicit arguments in each work, and discounted the life experience on which they were based. The great groundbreaking classic, *The Homosexual in America*, I dismissed because of its patently absurd supposition that most alcoholic men were latent homosexuals. Paul Goodman's essay on the great democracy of gay sex – that wildly tender encounter of strangers, brothers under the skin, stripped of distinctions of class, race and privilege of any kind, in the blessed anonymity of dark alleyways and hidden stairwells – I tossed aside as morally repugnant. One by one, I ticked off the items in my assignment, all the books and articles I had checked out of the library with embarrassment, mumbling and not making eye contact with the clerk. What had any of this to do with me, the meaning of my life, the great project I was embarked upon? I was at war with my body, my fallen nature, and this heroic struggle had the imprimatur of both the Christian and classical traditions. I was on familiar ground once more; I would be ready, brief in hand, for my last session.

I had gained a reprieve. The structure was intact. I felt relief. And gradually, inexorably, I began a slow slide into the longest, deepest depression of my life, three years in duration. I don't know that I termed it as such at the time; this was before the age of Prozac and Zoloft. In some ways my state of mind must have seemed a fulfillment of the general tenor of my life, a paralysis of will and sense of self-abasement so familiar and comfortable after all these years. Whatever I went through in that period, it was so bound up with the fabric of my life as to be indistinguishable from it. I couldn't imagine things being different; I couldn't imagine being happy or hopeful; I couldn't imagine, I could barely remember, the rambunctious, expansive young man of Llewellyn. Maybe that's what depression is sometimes, a failure of imagination.

I was committed to my marriage, that I knew. It connected me with my history and dreams and values, with the extended family that was so important to my growing up. Grandma and Grandpa, my aunt and uncle, Mom and Dad, my baby brother and I, we had all moved down from the Iron Range at the same time, in the late

Forties, living together as an intact clan for a year or more in a small log-cabin-style house on the northern outskirts of the Twin Cities, before dispersing and settling within a few miles of each other. Grandma and Grandpa dropped in at any time to visit, and all of us ate dinner together almost every Sunday, with the time spent in story-telling, fiery political arguments, philosophical discussions, and remembrances of life on the Range. How many times did I listen in rapt attention as Grandpa told about Jesus chasing the money-changers out of the Temple, inveighed against the Robber Barons of American capitalism, and castigated the Oliver Iron Mining Company for spying on its workers and drumming out the so-called communists, mostly Finlanders? And how many times did I hear him laud FDR for being the champion of unions and the savior of this nation during the Great Depression? It was heady stuff; I couldn't get enough of it.

Marriage was my entree into all of this, and more – a sense of high purpose and moral legitimacy. Besides, I wanted to be a father. Marriage was the rock on which I stood; all else was shifting sand. Was I depressed because I had low self-esteem, or did I have low self-esteem because I was depressed? Was I gay because I was depressed, or depressed because I was gay? In any case what did any of this matter? What mattered was doing one's duty, living up to one's responsibilities. The question of sexuality was moot anyway, for I barely had any sexual feelings to speak of. I was mostly impotent with Judy, though by a curious streak of honesty, I didn't consider it impotence. I didn't want to have sex with her.

The depression deepened and became its own reality, with everything around me both reflecting and reinforcing my inner emptiness. As I walked down the brightly lit corridors at my new job – technical editor at Control Data – I listened to the click of my heels on the slick floors and heard in the pulsing of fluorescents above me, in the thrumming of corporate life in the walls around me, all the energy and vitality I lacked in myself. Through office doorways I glimpsed workers consulting together on projects, down hallways I saw them visiting and laughing at the water cooler; they were happy, they knew the secret of life, I had lost it. Everything I saw and heard redounded to my discredit. The very walls, with their incessant humming, seemed to mutter as I passed, "You are false, a fraud, you have nothing to offer anyone, your life is a joke."

Slowly an idea began to take shape; I'm not sure when or how, or when I first put words to it. Judy had courted me aggressively, had broken down my defenses and drawn me out of my shell, and for that I was grateful. I could say, as I often did, I loved her, I cared for her, she was my best friend, and all these things were true; but with a core part of my being, in some private place I couldn't name or acknowledge, I withheld myself, I renounced her. Gradually, like a poisonous gas seeping up through the layers of a toxic waste dump, the idea crept into consciousness: "She is not of my choosing." I don't know what could have been of my choosing in that tormented, confused time; I had been given the chance to act and had balked. But there it came, rising out of the miasma of self-doubt and self-loathing, breaking through the crusts of accumulated denial and resentment, this one clear thought: "She is not of my choosing, not of my choosing." If I didn't have the courage to affirm my life's truth, at least I could achieve an integrity of negation.

We grew more and more estranged. One afternoon, I happened to meet her on the bus coming home from work; she usually drove. There was a vacant seat beside her but I hesitated in taking it; I felt intruded upon. Like strangers we sat silently beside each other, looking stiffly ahead, awaiting the reprieve of the familiar, isolating routines of home.

I had been given a formula by Dr. Thompson, then another at Llewellyn that stood the first on its head, a liberating truth which I ignored at my peril. How many signs would it take – how many dreams and crushes, how many stirrings of feeling and insight, how many depressions – before I would finally accept the truth of my nature? What would set me free?

Scuttling

The way down proved the way out. In the summer of 1978, still depressed, still impotent, I saw a third therapist, gay this time. I would engage the issue head-on; I had no other choice.

I was referred by a gay community services agency in Minneapolis. Just calling them, even looking up the number, was an ordeal: taking out the phone book and shoving it back, fingering through it and slamming it closed, lifting the receiver and banging it down, each gesture repeated over and over as I tried to snatch a moment's safety at work. I'd calculate when my office-mates were most likely to be gone for awhile, then shut the door, only to fling it open again, my heart thumping, as I lost my nerve or heard noises in the hall. Over and over again, for a couple of weeks this went on... only to be repeated for the call to the therapist.

David was a cute, short, stocky Irishman with a round face and pug nose who glided through his Queen Anne house on thick snow-white socks. The art on the walls, the sculptures on the cabinets, the books and magazines strewn about, sizzled with a casual homoeroticism all the more disturbing because it was domesticated, matter-of-fact. Had I crossed a frontier from which there was no return? My first assignment was to read and sign a statement stipulating that if by chance we should become attracted to one another, sexual relations were off-limits till a year following the end of therapy. I definitely wasn't in Kansas any more.

David's breezy manner disarmed me and I spilled my story easily. No need to couch my words or hide here; the taboos and mystique were dispelled. In the coming weeks and months, whenever I lapsed into my chronic defensiveness, he challenged me. He didn't have the same vested interest in the established order as my previous therapists – or as I did, for that matter.

When I dismissed my gay feelings by parroting Bruce's line that my lustful inclinations were probably no different from anybody else's, David looked at me with those wide, candid hazel eyes of his. "How would you know? You've never acted on them."

"You don't have to act on something to know about it. I don't need to murder somebody to know that murder is wrong."

"Why are you here then?"

When I echoed Dr. Thompson's line, brooding with that low hissing static of the analysand stuck in a maze of his own making – "Maybe my real issue is low self-esteem. That's what I should be working on. This gay thing is a ruse, a distraction" – he recalled my history.

"Hey, aren't you forgetting something, what you learned at Llewellyn?"

When I pitched the latest idea I had picked up from some book I was reading – like, "I don't think the issue is homosexuality per se. It's fear of sex, nonacceptance of my sexual nature. Homosexuality is just a fetish, a little piece I've broken off to make the bigger dread more manageable" – he was unimpressed.

"Hmmm... interesting – not my experience."

The issue for me was always something else, anything but the homosexuality. I was determined, invoking every argument I could think of to escape the inevitable consequence of the trajectory of my life.

In my greatest despair, backed against a wall, I would say, "The issue is really love – I can't love anybody. There's something fundamentally wrong with me."

Patiently, each time David brought me back to the reality of my feelings, my history, my identity since childhood, the reason I was there. And his counsel was always the same.

"You're probably going to feel stuck as long as this thing stays locked in your head. You need to get it out there, put it into action, to see what it means for you. Right now it's so huge and unimaginable, heaped and confused with so many other issues – your expectations and assumptions, your fears and fantasies, the baggage of your entire life – you don't have a clue as to what it really means. It could be a big nothing, or it could be the rest of your life. You won't know till you put it out there."

At some level I knew he was right but I was skittish and suspicious. He had an agenda, after all, as did the whole gay liberation movement, which was just then coming into its own. Gay House, a refuge for young people coming out, had been established in Minneapolis; the agency that referred me was initiating many support functions for the growing gay community; an openly gay man, Allan Spear, had been elected to the State Senate; efforts were underway to enact gay rights measures; Minneapolis had a gay paper; the University had elected Jack Baker student body president, and he had brought his lover up from Iowa, who hailed the crowd with a parody of the Black Power salute – limp fist raised high in the air. All this fascinated, and repelled me. What did I or my marriage, the struggle of my life, matter in this larger political context? I was just another recruit.

I didn't trust David. I didn't share with him the depth of my reservations; I didn't tell him about my daughter's same-sex feelings – I didn't think they were relevant; and when he suggested doing some couples counseling with Judy and me, I thought to myself, what does this guy know about marriage, how can he help? He just wants greater legitimacy.

Yet, deep down, I knew he was right. I knew that some day, somewhere, I would have to act on my feelings. But how? I had a gay friend, comfortably out, politically aware, happily connected with an older man in an established open relationship, and David suggested that I ask if he wouldn't be willing to have sex with me so I could see what it meant. I toyed with the idea briefly – I knew that Jon frequented the baths and that his partner had what were called "fuck-buddies" – but I discarded it as preposterous. Sex as experiment, recreation; sex as casual and matter-of-fact; sex stripped of romance or love, of complications and responsibility – the idea was repugnant, inconceivable. If this was the gay world, I wanted no part of it.

Though I fought David at every turn, there was a mysterious, powerful congruence between everything we were discussing and the two goals I had identified for myself early in the therapy. They had sprung to mind instinctively, fully formed, with no groping for words, as if the very act of deciding to seek help had given them birth. I didn't formulate them specifically in terms of the gay issue – probably resisted doing so – but the nexus was so clear that only a willful obliviousness could blind me to it.

In my first session I had told David that what I wanted, more than anything else, was to escape this paralysis, this sense of being a spectator at my own life, riding a roller-coaster of emotions over which I had no control. Also, I wanted to be able to love – as simple as that. The connection with the gay issue was so obvious as to be self-evident; the solution to the problem was implicit in its formulation. But I fought like hell not to see it.

Yet, despite my crab-like scuttle toward and away from my identity, the therapy set in motion a chain of events that within two years would lead to the dissolution of the marriage and my coming out as a gay man.

Home Free

What drew me to Gene more than anything else, was his knack for knocking me off-balance. Early at Llewellyn, before we became friends, he liked to steal into my office and crouch on his haunches behind me, sucking on his briar till I noticed him. He was exploiting his access as maintenance man, and I suppose my limited vision as well. He'd puff and puff till the sweet-sour fumes enveloped me and I tilted my nose to sniff the air; then it was back to reading page-proofs till the next assault. Sniff, sniff... It usually took several twitchings before reality dawned and I wheeled round to face my trickster.

"Not again, you rascal!" His head bobbed into view like Alice's Cheshire cat, his scraggly fringe of reddish-brown beard unzipped to flash a broad smile and his blue eyes glittered with satisfaction. The joke was on me – my single-minded obliviousness – but I relished these interruptions, and the talk that followed was like playing ping-pong with a whiffle-ball.

I made nothing of these escapades. Gene was gregarious; his push broom was a magic wand bringing chaos and merriment wherever he went. I could track its progress in the laughter that rippled throughout the production area. Then one afternoon as I left work late, crossing in front of the carriage house that served as shop and storeroom, I heard yelling behind me as I shuffled through the dry leaves in the alley on my shortcut to the bus stop.

"Hey, Bob, Bob!" I looked back to see him jumping up and down and waving his arms like somebody afraid of missing a train. "Where do you live? Maybe I could give you a ride, if you can wait a bit."

"No thanks, I gotta get home." In that brief exchange, however, for an instant I was yanked out of myself into something like a waking dream, vivid, immediate and timeless. I felt a tug in the breathless urgency of his voice, a flicker of recognition in our glance, and the timbre of his baritone resonated in the hollow of my chest like a low tuning fork; it reverberated all the way home, despite the clamor of my insistent questioning: what was happening here, what energy was I picking up, was this really coming from him or was it only more of my frustrated longing? This was crazy – he was straight as an arrow, a regular guy, an outdoorsman, a mechanic; he was dating a woman in accounting, for Christ's sake.

By spring my crush was rank with bloom. I was jealous of his attentions to the other employees, keeping score of slights, and on the many days when he was gone because of his other job or illness, I salved my loneliness by forging a friendship with his now live-in girlfriend... stalking by proxy. Ah, he likes sleeping late, drinks too much, hates broccoli, screams during nightmares about Vietnam, has to be pried out of his favorite shirt for washings on weekends. Details, details, my imagination was starved for details.

Then one morning in the break room we found ourselves alone sitting across from each other on straight-backed chairs, visiting about nothing in particular till he started talking about his frustration with work and his dream of becoming a professional astrologer. Physical labor was becoming painful due to a back injury sustained when he was blown out of a helicopter in Vietnam. As I leaned forward, sliding toward the lip of my chair, drawn by the conversation, taking him in, I felt an odd sensation at the base of my spine, an intense tingling. I shifted my weight but it spread, gathered force and began riding up my spine till it reached the base of my skull, where it penetrated, flooding my head, then my entire body with a rush. I tottered and grabbed the edges of my seat like a careening carnival ride.

"What's wrong?"

"Nothing, just got dizzy for a minute, that's all." I knew what it was, however... *kundalini.* We had recently finished production of a book called *Sexual Occultism* by an Australian yogi who was laying bare the secrets of Tantric yoga for Westerners interested in heightening and redirecting sexual energy to expand consciousness. "Better than LSD," he claimed.

If the gods had wanted to play a practical joke on me, they could not have picked a better banana peel than Llewellyn. It was a sexual zoo. My first day on the job, Gene and I hauled a dozen chairs down to the ritual room in the basement and he told me that the publisher, priest to a coven of witches, masturbated into the communion cup as part of the service. Every morning I trudged up the three flights of stairs to my office, walking past the second-floor landing outside the publisher's master bedroom suite, and saw the display cases full of sexual paraphernalia: handcuffs, manacles, leather hoods, whips, chains, shoes with seven-inch stiletto heels. One day we got an advisory from the publisher attached to the latest issue of *The Berkeley Barb*, whose front page featured a drawing of a monumental phallus surrounded and being climbed by hoards of adoring, orgiastic worshipers. "Why can't we have art like this?," the note read. Within hours the wags in advertising had produced versions of the image that popped up everywhere – on posters, flyers, brochures and toilet-seat covers. At Llewellyn sex was omnipresent; people wore it on their sleeves. The wife of the editor of our magazine, *Gnostica*, had begun life as Wanda, was Rusty when I first met her, and was about to undergo surgery to become David; Les, a man in shipping, was moving in the opposite direction and growing breasts. The keyliner had left her husband and was coming out as a lesbian, while our newest typesetter was a handsome young guy coupled with a man twice his age.

My defense was to take a professional attitude toward all of this, though it wasn't always easy. From our retail shop that sold pyramid hats promising everything from spiritual enlightenment to sexual potency, to working with the Moon sisters who channeled novels using a Ouija board hooked up to an IBM Selectric, Llewellyn blurred the line between fact and fantasy, chicanery and inspired genius. My job required equal parts suspension of disbelief and judicious discrimination. I was surrounded by witches, astrologers, palmists, tarot readers, New-Agers, pagans and psychics of all stripes. Gene himself was a devotee of *magick* with a *k*, not the innocuous white-bunny-pulled-from-a-hat variety but the sort practiced by Aleister Crowley, involving a discipline of self-transformation, the working of spells and the summoning of spirits and demons to manipulate reality. He had re-nounced it for the duration of a particularly nasty Saturn return. "Too risky," he said.

Despite their eccentricity, I admired the people at Llewellyn. Their lives had a certain integrity; they had been granted gifts and they followed wherever those gifts led. While I was definitely more open and expansive in my new job, I still held back. One day, while sitting at my desk reviewing my edits to his manuscript, the astrologer Noel Tyl commented on something he had seen in the horoscope he had cast for my job interview.

"With all those planets retrograde and clustered together in the upper hemisphere, you've got a lot of power locked away in your chart. No telling what you might accomplish if you tapped into it." For an instant I wondered if he was trying to smoke me out.

I knew Llewellyn was an invitation to a greater freedom, but I took refuge in my stance as objective ob-server, avoiding judgments, taking everything on its own terms. That's exactly the spirit in which I edited *Sexual Occultism*. Hmmm... *kundalini*, very interesting. Mentally I compared it and filed it away with more familiar phe-nomena – sexual ecstasy, the relation between the erotic and divine, Donne's Holy Sonnets, St. Theresa's mysti-cism – congratulating myself on broadening my horizons. Then, Whammo!, I'm nearly knocked off my seat by the sheer visceral force of the thing.

Gene and I start to become friends. Soon we're talking about taking fishing and camping trips together, then planning one for the following spring. Fishing opener in May finds us drifting lazily in my red canoe on a chain of lakes and ponds glistening under bright blue skies in the Chippewa National Forest of northern Minnesota. We pass the communal pint of dark Jamaican rum back and forth as bobbers and dragonflies dance beside floating carpets of green lily pads. The canoe rocks gently, sometimes tipsily, with every shift of our weight. We paddle from spot to spot, poling our way through shallow channels of reeds, as the sun drops low in the sky and begins popping through the darkening web of trees like a magnesium flare.

That evening in the tent – the air is close and full of the sweet tobacco-and-sweat smell of him – we talk like kids late into the night. He tells me about waking up in a body bag in a makeshift morgue in Nam and the near-death experience that gave him his psychic calling in life; he tells me about pointing a gun at his abusive stepfather, and stopping short of pulling the trigger; he tells me about a group ritual he led where the sacrificial chicken ran around the bonfire headless singing the "Star-Spangled Banner." I take it all in and am exhausted with the fullness of it – the day, the sun, the paddling, the talk, the lateness of the hour and the experience of this man.

Months later, after a second trip down a stretch near the headwaters of the St. Louis River, I joke to Judy that one sure way to kill desire is to dredge it in details. The mechanics of friendship between Gene and me are less than idyllic. We grate on each other in close quarters and often work at cross-purposes even in paddling the canoe, quarreling our way down the river.

Judy knows about the crush, knows it is one of the reasons I have gone to see Bruce for counseling. Despite my periods of coldness and withdrawal, and the rage and rejection simmering underneath, she is my best friend and confidant, the one person who knows my whole story. She is my one stay against the stark and lonely solitude of absolute secrecy. The crush – it has a life of its own. It ebbs and flows, flickers, occasionally flares through the scaffolding of my life. I watch it, study it. It is a pathology, my whole life is a pathology. It's all out there, separate from me, the watcher. Eventually the crush becomes part of the ordinary furniture of my life. Has this been my strategy all along, to domesticate *kundalini?* Or is some deeper wisdom at work?

One fall afternoon as we near the end of a day trip down a broad, majestic stretch of the Mississippi above Elk River, I am fatigued, my face is raw from sun and wind, and I am fed up with his continual strategizing.

"Aim for that 'v' up ahead, the darker, still place in the shimmering. Do you see it? That's where the main current is, that will carry us with the least resistance."

"Stop it, Gene. You're taking something I love, canoeing, and turning it into something I hate, chess." At his urging, we had taken up playing chess between trips. "I don't want to think my way down the river. What I like about canoeing is a lazy drifting, the rhythmic paddling, my body and arms moving in synch with the canoe and the water."

He patiently explains the deceptive power of the river, belied by its placid surface – like we're riding the back of a great serpent and have no choice but to work with and respect its energy. I know that he's right; I marvel at his practical, concrete wisdom, realizing that I am all abstraction.

The following April we're paddling the Rum River, aptly named for its crazy snaking through the midsection of Minnesota. The water is high and fast from the spring thaw, and at practically every crook in the river we must reconnoiter and strategize to negotiate the maze of fallen, criss-crossed trees, some of them submerged just below the surface. Paddling is arduous; my lake canoe is out of its element. It seems that Gene raises the stakes with every trip we take.

"Paddle right... left... right," he shouts from the back where he has the greatest control over maneuvering. "Hard right... right! Your other right! HARD right, god-dammit!" I'm in front with the quickest view of pressing danger. "Ease up, ease up! Back-paddle on the left, back-paddle!"

I see it too late – the delicate ripple traced by the current's caress against the barely projecting nub of a submerged tree. Powerless, I watch as in slow motion it hooks the front of the keel and glides along nearly half its length as we are shoved broadside with relentless force, and tipped up ever-so-gracefully, up into the air before being dumped unceremoniously into the water.

"Oh shit!," he yells. The cold hits like a mallet to the chest and knocks me breathless; I gasp, howling for air. Gene calls out from the other side of the capsized canoe to make sure I'm all right. Treading water in our life-jackets, we ease the craft to shore. Most of our goods are securely tied-in; towels and a change of clothes are packed in waterproof bags. We strip, dry off and dress, laughing at our adventure, grateful for our escape. I glow with new-found respect for this man.

He is a different breed from me. This strikes me one afternoon as he uncoils a hose in my driveway. I've hired him for some roof repair. He studies the pile for a minute as if to divine its deep structure, then picks an end and begins to tug and tease, waltzing with the tangle till it yields its secrets, unspooling its full, fluid length into his grip. I am amazed at the ease with which he does this; I imagine how I might have done it. I step boldly into the eye of the storm with one foot, straddle the coil heroically, seize the end that's nearest, then yank and pull, tug and curse, grabbing at loosening sections till they begin to loop themselves around my arms and legs and I am trapped like Laocoon in a snarl of snakes.

Driving back from the Crow River that summer, Gene begins to talk about porn movies, a favorite pasttime of his, to which he treats himself on birthdays. He won't let go; he describes threesomes he's seen, two women and a man, then two men and a woman, with the guys going after each other – a fantasy of his, he confesses. "I wonder what it would be like," and he looks at me. I take refuge in an old tactic of mine; I'm quiet, evasive and non-committal. "Oh"… "Really?"… "That's interesting"… This time, however, it all feels false. He's putting himself out there and I'm leaving him spinning in the wind. I'm a hypocrite, I think, not real or true with anyone. I feel with burning shame the lie of my life.

"Yeah, I can relate, Gene," I finally say. "I have a lot of those feelings too, they've dogged me my whole life. I've been in therapy twice before, and now I'm in it again. I used to have a real bad crush on you" – and here I look down at the door handle – "but you don't have to worry, I'm over it – it's O.K. now." Then I wonder, have I gone too far, assumed too much? Maybe this isn't what he meant at all, maybe the friendship is irreparably damaged – and for what?

"I've desired you five or six times," he says, looking me square in the eyes. I can't believe it. How could he feel the same as me? He's as straight as an arrow, a regular guy. Turns out, he's as kinky as a pubic hair.

That's the funny thing about loneliness, the feeling that you're alone in the universe. Rationally, you know it can't possibly be true, that there must be others like you out there. Until you've had your feelings reciprocated, however, validated by the response of another human being, until those feelings register in the world outside yourself, you might as well be the only one, like the proverbial tree that falls in the forest with no one to hear it.

Catching up on unspoken history, we drive fifty miles off-course. He tells me about feeling restless and hanging out at the adult bookstores downtown, one night getting the offer of a blow-job. "I don't know, I wanted it, but it didn't do much for me."

"Maybe because no feeling was involved," I say. It surprises me when he says the thought never crossed his mind. We agree that on our next trip, fishing opener next May, maybe we'll give it a try. We've got to be careful, deliberate; we have relationships to protect.

On that trip I am skittish, turned in upon myself. We drive all night, mostly in silence, so we can put in at dawn and fish all day. On the lake the line in my reel keeps snarling and Gene has to unravel it for me. I begin to think I hate fishing – the endless waiting and watching, the messing with tackle and bait, the blank expanse of water and sky. When we get to camp that evening, I'm mortified to discover that I've forgotten my sleeping bag. Gene chuckles, then makes me one out of blankets, a sheet and tarp. We grab a quick bite to eat at a roadside cafe, then it's more fishing, in the dark this time, from shore near a bridge. With his spotlight we can see the stupid things hunkering near the bottom of the channel, nearly motionless, thick as stones, their glassy eyes shining up at us. Minnows, grubs, worms, lures – nothing makes them stir.

By ten I've had it. On the drive back he puts his hand on my knee and my arms shoot up, fall back at the elbows, with my hands coming to rest clasping the base of my skull.

"I don't think I can go through with it, Gene."

"That's O.K., don't sweat it."

Sitting on the toilet before returning to the tent, my mind races. What am I doing, what will this mean? I will be utterly incompetent, out of my element, won't know what to do. It'll be worse than canoeing, me paddling left while he's paddling right. What if he has a forked penis like the Great Goat God he worships?

When I return, the tent is warm and cozy, pungent with the smell of marijuana. I sit beside him as we pass the pipe back and forth between us.   "O.K.?," he asks.

"Yeah."

"Take off your clothes." I strip down to my long-johns and he reaches for me. "Take those off!"

We uncoil from a sitting position into a near embrace, and as with Judy, the rest unfolds naturally. I know just what to do. I head for the "v", the dark place in the shimmering where the current runs deep and true, and we fit together as neatly as two pieces of a puzzle. *Ouroboros* – the serpent with the tail in its mouth. This continues for what seems like hours, though when Gene calls it a "marathon session" the next morning, I chide him with my penchant for exactitude, "Oh, Gene, you can't tell time accurately under the influence of pot." I am excited and hard, probably more turned on by what I am doing to him than by what he is doing to me, but who can say in a condition of pure reciprocity? I love the feel and smell of him, the coarseness of his skin, the mass and dynamism of his muscles, the push and pull between us, and though it sometimes throws me off-balance, this encounter with equal force, energy and initiative – aggressive, playful and tender by turns – thrills me. Then there's the exotic topography of body hair. When, reaching up between his legs toward the small of his back, I find a lush patch spreading just beyond the crest of his butt, I might as well be Columbus discovering the New World.

Something else is happening, however; I become aware that I can't feel anything down there. It's as if the wires have been cut. Several times I raise my head and stare into the darkness; Gene seems to be enjoying himself so I guess everything's O.K. What's wrong with me? Why can't I feel my body under someone else's touch? Judy never touched me there, not even when I asked – I'm the only one. Is my sexuality so strange and private, I can't share it with anyone? Will I be a failure as a gay man too? Fears and questions swirl at the verge of consciousness. The habits of self-negation don't vanish overnight. It will take me years to undo the damage that's been done.

This frenzy has to stop at some point, and I'm not going to come, so I tell Gene to fuck me and I roll over on my stomach. It's awkward and painful at first; I don't know why I'm doing this, it doesn't make rational sense to me. Yet somehow it feels right, it's what I have to do, the natural extension of my movement toward this man throughout the friendship – from my sliding toward the lip of the chair as I take him and his story in, to my listening intently that night on our first trip together. I take him in, bodily, all his energy, all his life-experience and stories, all his hopes and dreams, I take him in, and as I feel his excitement build, feel his rhythm catch, feel him drive into me with increasing focus and intention, all my sense of awkwardness and separation, of being ridden like an animal, with something on top of me pounding and pressing me down, squeezing the breath out of me, falls away and I am flying with him. At the penultimate moment he rears up, muffles a cry, then collapses in a rain of kisses on the nape of my neck. I am moved and fulfilled – could my own orgasm have been any more complete?

Later I will describe this experience to my first gay lover, a man very aware and articulate, who likes to boast of his "versatility," being that rare thing, a genuine top and bottom. With my love of abstraction I describe what moved me that night as "the collapse of the male principle, all that focused, driving energy and intention." Daniel knew exactly what I meant.

I am this curious mix of knowing and not-knowing. I seem to know what I need to do without knowing why I need to do it. My soul tells me where to go, when my mind doesn't know. It's odd, with all my fear and hesitancy about this first experience, I am perfectly clear on one point: somehow I know that the most important thing for me will be, not the sex, but how I feel when I look at him the next morning.

As I lie awake shivering in my makeshift sleeping bag, I take comfort in this knowledge, awaiting morning like a little boy eager to open his Christmas present. I'm a naked, quivering blob of protoplasm, all nerve ends and new life. I don't know if I'm shivering from cold, exhaustion or excitement, but I'm alive, I'm alive. Eventually, unable to sleep, I take my blankets and pillow into the car and curl up in the back seat.

The morning of the first day. Gene opens the door and he's pissed. "I told you to tell me if you got cold – why didn't you?"

"I didn't want to bother you."

"Well, you should've."

"Sorry." I appreciate his desire to watch out for me, but I've got this problem with independence. As I say my sorry, I look him square in the eyes. I like his pale face with its crooked nose. I'm calm and happy. I'm home free.

He's a perfect shit-head that morning. With my tunnel vision, I don't maneuver well in an unfamiliar environment and I depend on him to let me know how I can help. Usually, he's good about this, but this morning he's darting around me, zipping behind and in front of me, saying nothing, doing everything himself, leaving me to feel useless. I stand awkwardly to the side, sometimes rubbing my face, and I discover that I can smell him on my hands. To amuse myself, I do this more often.

"I can smell you," I say, putting my knuckles to my nose. "I like it."

He glares at me. "I don't know about you, but I plan on doing some serious fishing today." He can't touch me.

He's curt and dismissive as we drive to the lake, and makes a couple of disparaging references to my being a "fairy" and a "pansy." I start to wonder, maybe I went too far when I traced the whorl of his ear with my little finger, or when I bent to kiss the furry hollow of his chest. Yeah, that was weird, that was definitely crossing the line. The fucking and sucking, the stuff they do in the movies, that's all right, but the weird stuff I did last night… yeah, I suppose that makes me a pansy. But look who's talking. And the glimmerings of shame fall away before they can take hold. I am home free.

In the boat, under bleak grey skies, shivering in my jacket, as my reel snarls for the umpteenth time, I get really fed up. And I like smelling my fingers and I don't want them smeared with worm slime.

I yell out, and I don't care about the other boats around us, "I hate fishing. I mean I really, really HATE fishing." And I feel good.

"Yeah, well, I don't think I'm going to be taking you on any more trips." It's one of our fights. I sniff my fingers, and I'm happy, supremely happy. I'm home free, nothing can touch me.

COMING OUT

The Last Woman

At my request, Judy saw David once toward the end of my therapy with him, to better understand my issues and his proposed remedy, I assumed, but events took a turn. She cried through most of the session, she said later, and he got her to admit that she felt trapped in the marriage. Trapped, I thought, what does that mean? The rat! This is how he does marriage counseling?

Weeks later, in the fall, over glasses of Harvey's Bristol Cream, our favorite, she calmly, coolly proposed divorce. The marriage wasn't working, it was pointless to continue, she said. I was dumbfounded. I fought it with everything I had; I badgered, weaseled and cajoled. "What about Rachel?," I asked. I pleaded and promised to do better, and in the ensuing weeks – as if I could repeal unilaterally fourteen years of history – I put myself on my best behavior, applying what we had learned about family dynamics in therapy with Rachel. Communication improved, then in March Judy booked a tryst for us at the Lowell Inn in Stillwater, and wonder of wonders, the impotence was cured. "A miracle," I wrote in a letter to a friend, this renascence of family life rescued from the brink of ruin. Then in May, another miracle.

For months after the experience with Gene, I was incredibly horny with Judy, often having intercourse twice a day, in the morning and evening, until she complained, saying it was too much. I was crushed. I had finally come into my own sexually, was more ardent and expressive with her, less inhibited, and I thought that if she could grow along with me and lose some of her own inhibitions, no telling where the marriage could go.

She guessed the source of my energy. Just as I had told her about the crush on Gene, I had related his and my conversation in the car on the way back from the Crow River, reassuring her that if we ever did follow through, it would be an experiment only, sex without emotional or romantic complications, nothing to worry about. Then I told her what had happened in the tent.

"Stop, I don't want to know about this," she said, "I don't need to hear it."

"I've got to tell you," I said, "you have to know." To this day I can't say whether my insistence on rubbing her nose in the truth was a perverse form of honesty, the only integrity left to me in an otherwise impossible situation, or the most flagrant dishonesty, the distortion of a brain bifurcated by denial, this bland assumption that to me, all things were possible, this rudimentary failure to connect the dots of my life. Honesty, like denial, is a funny thing. Deep down I suppose *I saw* my fitful but continued disclosures as an effort to complete the sentence left hanging that night in the car when we first declared our love for one another.

It ate at me, her lack of responsiveness in lovemaking. It was a long-standing issue, and every time I raised it, I got the same answer. But this time, in the flush of new ardor, tasting possibility, I pressed for clarification.

"Why don't you come with me?"

Once again came that cryptic answer, now uttered more definitively: "Maybe if I desired you more..." That unfinished sentence, so fraught with the unspoken – what did it mean? This time, unlike all the other times, I didn't let the matter lie, dissipate in noncommittal silence.

"What do you mean exactly?" And I pushed her, question by question, for definition, explanation, history.

"Stop. You're making me say more than I want to." Coolly, dispassionately, with lawyerly skill, I pressed on, drew her out, checked statements, getting clarification and corroboration, until everything was out in the open, the whole stinking lie of my life: she didn't trust me, we weren't a real family, she didn't desire me, we'd have to find fulfillment elsewhere.

It was over. I stormed out of the house into the sweltering July evening and walked for hours without purpose or direction, until my feet were raw and my mind was exhausted from endless recapitulations of meaningless history. Was I angrier at Judy or myself? I pounded out my rage on the pavement, as if stomping the dirt of my life off my shoes. We lived just a mile and a half from where I had grown up, and I walked past the fields where I had played as a boy, now filled with tract homes; past Lee Elementary and Regent Junior High, now a residence for seniors and a community center; past my old neighborhood, past the house where Arizona and I had lain on his bed ogling the girls across the street; past the railroad crossing near Triangle Park where Denny Nelson had told me he hoped that some day I would know the transforming love of a woman; past all the landmarks of my growing up. They barely registered. My childhood was a closed book. Everything had lost its particular significance and flashed by in a blur of aching, indefinite nostalgia. I walked and walked until I couldn't walk any longer, couldn't think or feel any more.

"I'm the last woman you'll ever really love." Judy said this not with triumph but more sadness than anything else, and perhaps with a shock of recognition. We were living together until it was convenient for her to move out. She thought it would be best for Rachel and me to stay in the house, me because of my growing blindness, and Rachel because of school, friends and her attachment to grandma and Grandpa, who lived a few doors away. Besides, Judy wanted a fresh start.

We were seated at the dining-room table after dinner – Rachel was outside playing – and I was telling her how Debbie, a close friend at work, had written me off. "Just like that," I said, hurt and baffled.

"I wondered if the friendship would last, if she could take the tension." Not in a hundred years would I have made the connection. Women were like that, I thought, able to divine the heart of the matter in a flash. She grasped that Debbie loved me as more than a friend and when she realized that we would never be more than that, she took a simple quarrel between us and magnified it into full-blown estrangement through a campaign of chilly, unforgiving silence. Debbie and I were barely speaking at work any longer, except to conduct business.

When I had first told Debbie that Judy and I were divorcing, then said I was gay, she cautioned me, drawing on an earlier conversation of ours, "Oh, don't jump to any conclusions, Bob. You've been dissatisfied in the marriage; you're just sexually unfulfilled. Now both you and Judy will have a chance at fulfillment."

Why were people always telling me I wasn't gay? I used to listen, drawing reassurance from their words, but no more. When I came out to my parents, Dad had said, "You just haven't met the right woman yet."

"No, Dad, that's not it, I've always been this way. No woman is going to make any difference; Judy was my best shot." Mom, as usual, got it; she had inklings from the start.

"Don't you remember, Rob, when he was eleven, talking about taking him to see the doctor about it?" Dad didn't remember, didn't have a clue.

I met Debbie's dismissal of my feelings with my own internal dismissal of her remark. I knew where I stood, had never been so clear about anything. She hadn't understood, but Judy did.

"I'm the last woman you'll ever really love."
"Yes, that's right," I said.

I had met Debbie two years earlier when she joined the public information staff at the Minnesota Department of Education, where we quickly grew from colleagues to friends. She was bright, literate, creative, full of fun and a sense of adventure. Both readers, we relished books, writers and language, trading favorites and sharing passages. She had this way of marching across the reception area and planting herself in my doorway – no escape – leaning jauntily against it with her short, broad frame, her arms folded across her chest and her perfect, pretty oval of a face cocked in anticipation.

"Entertain me!" I had no choice; she wouldn't tolerate my passivity, my habit of listening and reacting. She demanded engagement. I put myself on full display, and – surprised at my performance – basked in the approbation of her beaming smile, which spread across her face and reconfigured everything in the room around itself. That beatific smile – it was so open to life and full of expectancy, so radiant with joy, and so different from Judy's averted, self-protective gaze. I greeted it, came to depend on it, like the rays of the rising sun. It was magical, this friendship of ours, an unexpected gift in a stingy, unforgiving time, and as it developed I imagined we would always be friends, I assumed it like a condition of my existence. It was destined.

It was about as close to falling in love as you can get, without actually falling in love. For me, that is, not Debbie. At some point in the friendship, months before our fight, after a particularly close time together at her place, we were talking on the phone and she said she loved me, had felt strongly attracted the first day we met and was relieved to learn I was married, precluding one of those messy office romances. Inexplicably, the phone went dead. I called back and said I loved her too – but more casually, yet as if I were saying the same thing, hoping to defuse the situation. I did love her, but as a friend. I would have considered myself blessed to be best-buddies with her for the rest of my life, the way I was with Margo – always free and open, able to share almost anything with perfect spontaneity and frankness. I could have such intimate friendships with women because I enjoyed them and felt such an affinity with them... and sex was out of the picture.

It was a reprise of the friendship with Judy, that mutation of closeness into a sense of inevitability, but this time I was clear about who I was and what I wanted and had the courage of my convictions. So when Debbie turned the screws for a deeper intimacy, as Judy had done, I was immune. I was a different man. And Judy, at some level, grasped all of this in a single insight that took my breath away.

"I'm the last woman you'll ever really love." Not even I, with all my driving energy and clarity of purpose, would have then dared to make so sweeping a pronouncement. This life of mine was so new, unknown. In retrospect I can describe my thoughts and actions in deliberate terms, but the clarity exists mainly in hindsight. I acted with emerging awareness and intention, as much out of sheer instinct as anything else, the instinct for fulfillment and self-realization liberated that night with Gene. Survival instinct? A life-force had been tapped.

"Yes, that's right." And I understood it as she understood it. I like to think she got it almost before I did, the full and life-changing import of this act of freedom. For all the ways in which I had hurt her, in which my struggle had hurt us, she was my friend and confidant and knew my story better than anyone. In that moment at least, she looked past her own hurt and saw to the heart of the matter. She grasped that my gayness went beyond occasional feelings and attractions, beyond fits of restlessness and yearning, perhaps beyond feeling and desire. It went to the core of identity.

It's a loss when a marriage unravels, even one as imperfect as ours. All the hope, energy and idealism of youth, the shared history of building a future together, the countless rededications required to keep the marriage alive, come to nothing. For me the loss was compounded.

I did not get to give that rare thing, my first love, to a man – I will never have that experience; and the love I gave to Judy was in part withheld and given grudgingly. I can only imagine the toll this must have taken on her. I'm not referring only to the rages, withdrawals, the coldness, my treating her like a stranger sometimes; nor to my riding her about her appearance, how she should lose weight, dress or wear her hair to please me; nor to my poking fun at her body – her "murderer's thumbs" for example. I'm referring to a more subtle, pervasive kind of rejection. Early in the marriage, shortly after we had set up house-keeping, when she excitedly proposed having lunch to-gether regularly at the university, I responded coldly, "We see each other every night." It was the tone. With some part of my being – I was only half-aware at the time – I saw something begin to die in her eyes, the sense that we were in this together, in the same spirit.

Another look haunts me. It was the first year of the marriage and we were still getting used to the me-chanics of regular love-making. She made a move on me in the middle of the night, and without knowing why, I got hysterical and started screaming, "Don't ever do that again!" She left the bed and went into the living room and I chased after her, yelling, "Don't ever do that again, don't ever expect anything of me that way, do you un-derstand?" Who was this raging night creature escaped from his lair, so bent on survival, who towered over her, trembling and shaking his fists in the air, as she sat cow-ering on the couch, looking up at him with her eyes full of fear and incomprehension? We never spoke of that night.

If my friend Earl in the Fathers' Group could weep for withholding a part of himself from his wife, I could weep a thousandfold. He had been faithful, a true friend; he had nursed her through a long illness before she died, and then come out at age sixty-five. He had withheld only one thing, but it was crucial, the knowledge of who he truly was. "She must have known and it must have hurt her," he had said on two different occasions in group, breaking down and sobbing. If he could weep for that, I could weep a thousandfold. There was no way to make amends for this. "After such knowledge, what forgiveness?," Eliot writes in one of his poems.

It has taken me years to grieve the marriage. The last major piece – over the injury to Judy – I didn't begin to let go of till ten years after the divorce. On at least two occasions I had tried to make amends, but she wouldn't hear of it – she's as relentless about forgetting the past as I am about recovering it. I went to a counselor who happened to be a spiritual director, and told her my grief. She said that Judy was a part of what had happened, she had bought into it and helped sustain it for whatever reason. I didn't buy her explanation exactly – it seemed to let me off the hook too easily – but the act of confessing and receiving a kind of absolution helped me to begin to let go, and I have come to believe there's a deep wisdom in acknowledging the mutuality of our condition, that what happens, happens between us, and I take comfort in this. It is part of empathy, for myself as well as others, part of rejoining the human race.

It has taken me a long time to grieve the marriage, and I'm still working on it. In a flash I can revisit a scene and uncover some forgotten hurt, or see afresh in a familiar memory some facet of a wrong I had overlooked. This isn't morbid; I'm not stuck in the past. It's healing; as I remember, I let go. I'm owning my life, all of it.

Maybe it's like near-death experience. People who

have technically died and then revived sometimes report traveling through a dark tunnel and coming into the presence of an all-loving light. Often slighted in popular accounts is a darker side of the experience: the life-review. They see their entire lives laid out before them, not highlights, but everything they've ever done or thought or said, good and bad, all at once, and they see the totality of those actions, including all the repercussions on others through time. The experience can be almost unendurable, and would be so except for the presence of that all-forgiving light, which allows them to stand in the truth of their lives. I sometimes wonder if I'm getting an early start – maybe because I need the extra time! This feels right, this standing in the light of my life and owning everything. The memoir is only the most visible and outward sign of this work.

Judy and I lived together civilly for the five months it took her to move out, but it was an awkward, painful time, full of bitterness, resentment an occasional hoping against hope that some arrangement could be worked out – maybe I could hole up in the basement –to keep us together for Rachel's sake. One night as we were talking, recounting our history together, Judy expressed her own remorse. She looked at me and said as she started to cry, "I'm afraid I made you a homosexual."

"No you didn't. I've been this way since I was a little kid."

For two or three months after she left, I couldn't bear her intrusions into the house, to get her things or to pick up Rachel. I froze with an angry static, bristled if she came near. I wanted her wiped off the face of the earth; I imagined her as an oily slick on the highway.

Then it lifted. As I told family and friends at the time, I peeked around the corners of my bruised ego and maybe for the first time in my life saw her for who she really was, a person in her own right, with her own identity and needs, independent of me and all my projections onto her.

The marriage ended where it began. We became good friends all over again, this time with a greater candor and reality, sharing the most intimate parts of our lives, her discovery of her sexuality, my discovery of mine. Debbie was right; we were finally finding fulfillment. We had so much to talk about after all – we both loved men.

Loving Men

When I came out to my family, my sister-in-law Mary reacted with surprise and her typical candor. "But Bob, I thought you liked women."

"I do, but I'm attracted to men."

In explaining my feelings to Debbie and my qualms about embarking on this new adventure – we were still friends at the time – I said, "It's funny, I'm attracted to men but I'm not sure I like them very much, not the way I like women. I admire and enjoy women, feel close and connected with them. I'm not all that comfortable with men."

Debbie glowed. "I always knew you had good taste."

In coming out I have learned to like men; in the process I have come to like and accept myself as a man, and discovered a talent for friendship with men.

When Judy left the house on December 1, 1980, I decided to inaugurate this new stage in my life by hosting a dinner party for my closest friends. Six women. Despite the good intentions, the dynamics were peculiar: six single women with no connection other than their closeness with me, a newly singled man who was wholly unavailable. What were they supposed to do, vie for my favor? Say what you will about diversity, new social and sexual roles and the creation of flexible institutions to accommodate this reality, the party was a bust. Awkward, static, stilted. Sexual basics are hard to budge.

I had no male friends to invite. There was Barry, as far as I knew the only other conservative in the mostly liberal education department; we met conspiratorially in the basement cafeteria to discuss Reaganomics. Another guy, who used to be in advertising at Llewellyn, would take me to strip shows where he'd get tanked and open up to me; I wondered if he was one of those closet-cases who needed alcohol as a cover and release. I had a kind of friend, an interesting older guy I had met recently, married and closeted, with whom I occasionally had recreational sex – quickies (he was always hurrying home to the family). I admired the close attachments he had managed to form with his straight male friends – it was a freedom he claimed for himself – but I was sad to see him restless, always on the lookout, left wondering in any encounter with a man, whether camping with a buddy or chatting with a friendly stranger at the Y, was this guy interested, was something possible here; then afterward, when he failed to act, the lingering regret.

I was surprised to learn that Debbie also had a special friend; she confessed with some embarrassment that he sometimes stole onto her porch at night and tapped on the windows. Their names gave us hysterics: Randy and Dick. The gods were laughing at us.

I couldn't have invited Gene to the party, and in any case we had drifted apart. We had taken one last fishing trip in the fall, to Lake Pepin – more than a year ago now – where we exchanged blow-jobs leaning against a tree in a field of stinging nettles, four and five feet tall, blasted black by an early frost. We flipped a coin to see who would go first, and when I got the call and went down on him, he shot me a look. I didn't know there was a script; I was only doing what came naturally. This exchange followed months of no contact after our time in the tent, several phone calls of mine that he hadn't returned and a conversation in the canoe just prior to the exchange where I had tried to express some of what I felt for him. For, despite the terms of our arrangement, I was getting attached. "Be careful, those are dangerous words," he had said. I have to confess, the sex didn't do much for me, maybe because, as I had told him in another context, no feeling was involved.

I got a wedding announcement in the mail several months later showing him in a white jacket looking dapper standing next to his new bride, a woman he had never mentioned. Mike had married Susan shortly after our time in Madison. What was it with these guys that they had to run off and get hitched just when you were getting close? I sent a classy gift and a congratulatory note, which mentioned my own news. He was furious when he called; his wife, who knew about our trips, had given him the third degree.

"You got me in a lot of trouble." He was dismissive of the most important decision of my life. "Why do you have to go and do that? It's not necessary."

"Maybe not for you." And with that response, I wrote him off. Perhaps I did lack discretion, wasn't considerate enough of other people's feelings. It was a heady, celebratory time for me; I was telling anyone who would listen, even strangers at the bus stop. I had been super-discreet my whole life. At what cost? Let others bear the cost of my indiscretion now. I would be myself.

This energy of coming out – it was rushing through me, transforming everything. It was raw, brutal and divisive; it divided the old me from the new me, false friends from true, words, thoughts and impulses that undermined my cause from those that advanced it. It set me apart from my family, wrecked friendships, ended a marriage, alienated me from my society and culture. And I didn't care. What I had dreaded all those years, what had kept me imprisoned in a life that wasn't my own, it was all coming true, and I didn't care. This surge of new life – I would ride it like a rushing torrent, gladly go wherever it led. I accepted the consequences of my actions because this was my life, I owned it.

My not having close male friends was nothing unusual; it's true for many men, for a variety of reasons. The twist in my case was my discovery with my seventh-grade shop teacher that closeness with my own sex could lead to dangerous complications, the development of tender and romantic feelings. So I distanced myself from boys I knew and formed intense attachments with near-strangers who came to life only in imagination. A second twist, another defense, was that, having concluded I was not like other men, I concocted my own private notion of masculinity, which set me apart from ordinary men and made me identify strongly with women, to the extent that I saw myself as their champion in the battle with the more brutish, doltish sex. This was self-hatred compounded, and hardly a recipe for closeness with men.

I liked women, felt simpatico and could open up easily with them; they were sensitive, aware of their feelings and able to verbalize them; they valued close relationships and communication. I could admire their beauty, charm, intelligence and wit; I could appreciate their delicacy of feature, smoothness of skin and grace of movement, but it was all out there, as if I were looking through a pane of glass. The wellsprings of desire were absent – the urge to know, possess or merge with them – maybe because the feminine was already highly developed within myself. Who knows?

Men, on the other hand... ah, men. A man will move me in a way that a woman won't. That's as close as I can come to describing what makes me gay, that quality of being moved. It includes but goes beyond physical attraction, the fascination with the look, shape, feel, sound, smell and movement of a man; it extends to his speech, gestures, energy, attitude and manner of engaging the world; and then it takes a further leap to something more intangible still, a hunger or yearning for the soul or essence of a man.

I am generalizing grossly here, trying to put words on the ineffable. For me that male essence is in part a quality of hurt, vulnerability, wounded ness, a softness buried beneath a crust of toughness, some recess that can be reached or breached only through love. I suspect that this quality that attracts me to men is similar to what attracts many women to them. And vice versa – many men are drawn to the vulnerability in women, which touches them to the quick.

In cruising the personals ads, I liked seeing a favorite of mine pop up from time to time. The headline read, "Lone Wolf." I don't know if it was the same guy each time – it appeared over several years – or some archetypal man speaking through many brothers. I never answered the ad, but to me it expressed an aspect of the male condition. A lone wolf, a deeply social creature separated from the pack, needing his distance but craving community, circling endlessly a world just out of reach – I encountered this ambivalence, paradox, call it what you will, in many of the men I met, acted out in countless ways, intricate dances of attraction and repulsion. It is not all negative, this bi-polar energy; it allows men to form bonds with each other that are close and deep, but more loosely affiliated than traditional marriage.

My dad had some of this lone wolf in him. A good father and family man, definitely present for my brother and me throughout our growing up, he nonetheless possessed an untouchable solitariness. My picture of him is of sitting alone on the front stoop under the stars at night, nursing a beer and smoking his pipe; or of getting up early on Saturday mornings when he could do his chores to the songs of birds, with nobody else around. In later years he took his meals alone in his chair, away from the dinner table, and once when he tried to push it even further by taking his plate into his lair, the basement – the drinking had become serious by then – Mom had to draw the line. That untouchable quality, that solitary strength in reserve, that shadowy, elusive presence at the edge of my awareness, stalking the fringes of communal life – that's part of what draws me to men.

Now, I freely admit this smacks of pathology, but it is my pathology and I own it. It is part of who I am and how I love; anyone who thinks love is devoid of pathology is probably deluded. There is a sickness, a brokenness in all of us that needs to be healed, and in being drawn to it, we heal ourselves. The miracle of love is how that pathology is transmuted into a creative, generative force.

Ever since I was that little boy lying in bed at night trying to retrieve that dream from a time almost before memory – of setting forth on a heroic journey to find and heal my sick uncle in a land far away – I have known what set me apart and made me special: that opening of tenderness to a man. Whatever lies I told myself or others, however much I might forget myself in assuming so conscientiously the roles assigned by social convention, that simple truth remained, preserved through dream and memory, immune to all the machinations of my mind and will. It kept me clear where I was going and finally called me home.

Daniel Folding Clothes

I watched Daniel sort and fold clothes with a flair and theatricality, an expressiveness that perfectly captured the drama of the moment, infusing every gesture with his personality and imagination. His only props were the clothes in the basket before him, tangled in a patchwork of rich reds and blues, pastel pinks and greens; satiny briefs in salmon, teal, burgundy and cream; tufts and knots of practical, luxurious cotton and sleek synthetics. Let loose like birds from his large tapered hands, they shimmered in the warm glow of the lamplight as he shook out the wrinkles and static before folding each piece neatly and stacking it in tidy piles on the bed we sometimes shared.

With my limited tunnel vision, I zoomed in on the scene like a movie director, savoring every detail. I watched with amazement – Daniel, my first real brush with the gay world. Newly out at age 38 after sixteen years of marriage, and still vested in that dream and clinging to a mostly conventional, respectable persona, I was nonetheless eager for this new adventure. Daniel had gone around the world on me" the first time we went to

bed, nibbling and sucking on every part of me in relentless succession, and I was his. What could I do but call
him two days later and tell him shamelessly, "I'm in
love"? I couldn't eat, I couldn't sleep and I paced the floor
for hours with my mind racing. For the first time in my
life, I understood, I resonated with the lyrics of popular
love songs. "Fly me to the moon," "Baby, do it to me one
more time," even the most banal of lyrics – now they
spoke for my experience too.

Daniel had carried the basket of clothes the way I
would have, slung cavalierly in front of his right hip,
walking with a stride and swagger that belied the weight
of his burden. He hefted it neatly onto the bed with a
graceful arch of his back, a nudge of his thigh, and one
long easy swing of his thick, strong arms. His stocky six-
foot frame, big-boned and broad-shouldered, nevertheless had a feminine quality: round, sensuous, even volup-
tuous, with a smooth sheath of fat softening with folds
and dimples the angular geometry, the rough junctures
and ridges of the male body. "Rubenesque," he liked to
call himself, patting his ample belly and hips. His face
had a similar indeterminacy, not so much androgynous
as suspended intriguingly somewhere between boyhood
and manhood; in the same light, almost in the same instant, with the flash of a gesture or look, he could turn
from banker to cherub, from the serious father of two
nearly grown sons to wickedly seductive waif.

It was his habit sometimes, when he came to stay
with me on those weekends when my daughter was at
her mother's, to bring his wash. All business at first, he
dipped into the basket, taking out each piece quickly and
crisply, snapping it in the air before folding and stacking
it with almost military precision. But as I watched, lean-

ing my weight against the doorjamb, he couldn't help himself; he got caught up in the spectacle of fabric and color, their shimmer and play in the muted pink light of the room, and like a priest or magician, began to raise each piece into the air with a flourish, delicacy or abandon – whatever the genius of the moment called for – and commend it to the ether as if with a blessing on its essential nature. In his hands, the fabric was alive. In folding it, he caressed it, charmed it into submission, coaxed it to lie smooth and still like a kitten on the bedspread.

I stared, delighted, fascinated with the full range of feeling and expression available to this man, his ability to glide easily along the spectrum from bluff machismo to the exquisitely feminine, unconstrained by convention or the expectations of others. And I grew sad. His freedom and completeness moved me; I felt a loss, an emptiness. Where was the fey boy of my childhood? Barely a trace remained in the staid, responsible man who now stood framed in the doorway, composed like a completed work, his focus fixed, his arms folded tightly across his chest, his left leg crossed precisely over his right shin, his whole body stiff and wooden. Why was it that, no matter what the pose, standing or sitting, I could feel myself locking into some gesture, freezing as if in a premonition of rigor mortis? Why did I feel I lugged my body from place to place like a dead weight, as if somehow separate from myself?

"I admire your freedom and expressiveness," I told him later over cups of steaming tea as we sat at the dining-room table. He drew his lips into a sweet bow of a smile. I wondered aloud about the boy I had been, who now seemed lost to me forever. Once he had claimed as his birthright that same freedom and expressiveness, but

I had sold him out, disowned him in a squalid deal for acceptance and legitimacy. Now I could barely glimpse him through the mists of memory, the distortion of years of accumulated judgment and censure.

"Let's go to bed," he said, taking my hand. I wasn't sure I wanted to have sex; sometimes I just wanted to be close to a man; most of the time, newly out, I barely knew the difference. Tonight, I thought I did, and I felt hesitant. For me, the love-making that followed, like the conversation, was in a minor key, full of loss and nostalgia, but Daniel entered into it with his usual zest, pronouncing afterward, "I LOVE sex – I have never known such desire." It thrilled me, but scared me too, this relish and abandon. I remembered the first time I had embraced and kissed a man while standing; it had almost knocked me off my feet. I'm not talking passion and excitement here, just practical mechanics. In my marriage I was used to being the guy in charge, the initiator, the one possessing superior weight and strength, and sex between me and my wife was usually reserved and polite. With guys, it was a whole different ball-game.

I lay there, under his weight, as if separate from my body, drifting away, in and out of the moment. "I feel like a castaway lost at sea, unsure if I'll ever find land," I said, not looking at him.

He raised himself slightly and said, "It's got to be hard, coming out after all those years of marriage, never being able to be yourself. You don't have to be afraid, I'll be here for you." I relaxed into the comfort of his arms, reassured for the moment, and let my thoughts drift to the boy of long ago, racing through the stinging grass in the hot dog-days of August, his pants-cuffs crusted with sandburs, sweat plastering that horsy forelock of hair against his forehead, running free through the woods and fields of an enchanted childhood.

As it turned out, Daniel wasn't there for me as I scrambled ashore. That was just one of many lessons I would learn in coming out: the incredible freedom and fluidity of gay relationships. After years of being sexual with only one person, my wife, strictly within the conventions of monogamous marriage, in a few years I was pitched headlong into a parallel universe, with its own myths, values and rules. I, who had never dated in high school or college, who came to marriage a virgin, was answering personals ads, having one-night stands, making a stab at serial monogamy with a string of boyfriends and lovers, exploring sex with multiple partners, engaging in organized orgies with Tantric religious overtones, and most fantastically of all, enjoying sexual friendships, that is, physical intimacy with men who were my friends and who remained my friends despite the sex, with almost no romantic complications. I could not have imagined such a world before entering it, and nothing in my prior life had prepared me for it.

I was lucky to have Daniel as my first lover. He was sexually experienced and a wise and patient teacher; he was politically aware and totally comfortable with himself as a gay man. He had known about himself from age five, had nevertheless tried marriage twice, and when I met him, he had just broken up with his male partner of ten years, with whom he had shared a home and a business. In the two or three months we were lovers – which I thought would last a lifetime, and he more wisely termed "our affairlet," having more words for the varieties of love than Italians have for pasta – he taught me the ropes in bed, including the rules of safer sex, which probably saved my life in the plague to come. Through him I met older men who had been out for decades and called each other "sister"; I met drag queens, cross-dressers, bull-dykes, lipstick lesbians, men in the process of becoming women and women in the process of becoming men, and other men like Daniel and myself who had been married and led fairly ordinary lives. I entered a counter-culture with its own manners and mores, its own arts and aesthetic, its own politics and spirituality, its own history and vernacular. Mostly, through Daniel, I learned there WAS land on the other side of this perilous crossing.

I remember the first time I went to a gay movie as a man on the verge of coming out, just before I met Daniel but months after my wife and I decided to separate. It was a quality film, German with subtitles, *Die Consequenz*, about two men who fall in love in prison. I took a seat way in the back of the theater, with lots of empty seats around me, and slouched down as far as I could in my seat, letting my jacket collar ride up around my ears to hide my profile. In front of me flickered the grainy images on the screen, exciting and disturbing at the same time; behind me I heard the shrieking and cackling of queens. I wondered, Were these my only choices? I didn't know. What could I expect, what would become of me if I took this leap into an unknown future? From Daniel, I learned there was a brave new world out there, full of choices, with much of the territory already mapped, and plenty of room to chart my own course. So, in a sense, he was there for me after all.

There was a trickier passage to navigate, however, an interior one, and although Daniel provided a model of self-acceptance, and blessed me not only with that but with his total acceptance of me, he could not show me how to get there. Some things you have to discover for yourself. Although Daniel had made the transition from marriage to gay life successfully, and had come out whole, it would take me years to do the business of grieving – letting go of a certain dream of myself, making my peace with loss and hurt, and flying free. Grieving and freedom, letting go and becoming whole, these were the journeys for which there were no maps or mentors. I was on my own.

Blessed Fraternity

"We're adequate," he says, comparing his with mine, mine with his. I had felt awkward undressing in a lit room. "ADDD-equate," he purrs again, drawing out its first broad syllable, caressing the word as lovingly as the thing itself. No novice, he's been around the block more than once, and now, he announces, is about to go "around the world" on me.

"Lie back. Enjoy. You don't have to do a thing. Men always think they have to do something back." I get performance anxiety about not having to perform.

It lies there limp, immune to all his tender ministrations, my poor orphan penis, shrunk with the freight of unspoken expectation; untouched, unloved I thought, through sixteen years of marriage, by anyone but me. Understandable perhaps. It's an awkward thing, really, unmentionable in polite conversation, graceless, wayward, with a mind all its own, but usually dutiful when pressed into service. A good soldier.

But, well... "Small"... there, I've said it. "Small." Or so I've always thought, till tonight, perhaps confusing issues of size with issues of shame, when maybe the issue was something else entirely. It was best kept under wraps, this thing, taken out under cover of darkness, or simply under covers. In locker rooms, surrounded by other guys, I always turned to the wall to drop my shorts, lose my shame in the shadows, and in the showers, with their brazen light, I dropped my gaze, like a kid playing hide-and-seek who thinks, "If I can't see them, they can't see me."

"ADDD-equate," he coos again. "I like it that we're both the same size," he says. Same size? His looks so big. And then he proceeds to list all the things he likes about my body, things I hadn't even noticed, like my skin, my hair, my hands, the high arch of my foot.

"Your mouth, your tongue, a dew-filled orchid," he had said when I had gone down on him. My wife and I, we hardly ever spoke during sex, but this guy, he's a regular chatterbox.

I watch it lie there in the pink lamplight, perverse with its own imagination, as if it didn't belong to me. And he goes around the world on me, sucking on fingers, toes and ears, bony knees and smelly armpits, the tender, blue-veined hollow on the inside of my elbow, blessing every undistinguished part of me, with a wicked deliberation, like a child tonguing a popsicle to a delicate point on a hot summer day. He French-kisses some spot on my belly, just inside the cup of my hipbone, and I moan. "You didn't know about that one, did you?"

"ADDD-equate," he croons again, having completed the circuit, then goes down on me. Yes, a dew-filled orchid. And with that one long, languorous, luxurious kiss, bestowed as lovingly as the syllables of his benediction, I am received irretrievably into the blessed fraternity of men who love men.

Friendship

I was lucky, I came out into a ready-made family. Lots of guys don't have this luxury; for them coming out can be a restless cruising through the bushes, a late-night haunting of the bars, a traipsing from party to party, a lonely, luckless trolling through the personals ads. Not to disparage any of this – it can all be a rewarding part of the adventure – but repeated too many times, with nothing more substantial growing out of these encounters, one can be left feeling empty and adrift, more alone than ever. The hunger for companionship, family and community that lies at the heart of this searching is not assuaged, only sharpened.

I was lucky, I stumbled into a ready-made family. I was introduced to The Fathers' Group by a man I met through a personals ad in *The Advocate*, a national gay magazine. The ad said he was looking for a "quality one-to-one relationship" with a guy "unafraid of intimacy." I was his man, but by the time I met him – a tall, lanky professor of textile engineering with coolly appraising milky blue eyes and an unruly yellow-grey mustache that bristled like a worn wire brush – he and his much younger lover were back together again for the third or fourth time, having negotiated a six-month contract stipulating terms, expectations and goals, complete with escape clauses. He had to honor that commitment, he said, but looking me over, added, "Maybe after the six months are up..."

The Notorious Doctor Bob, as he later became known in local and national S&M circles, took me to my first meeting of the Fathers' Group, where I quickly felt at home. With the exception of my escort, the dozen guys in their late-thirties to late-fifties were men like me, conventional family men, college-educated and professional, each struggling to affirm his same -sex feelings within the context of being a family man. Some were newly separated and in the throes of coming out; some were determined to stay married, hoping to find some accommodation or compromise that would grant them peace of mind; others sat on the fence or flip-flopped from meeting to meeting.

We met on the fourth Saturday of each month for a pot-luck and group discussion. Several of the men were veterans of counseling or were graduates of a group for gay or bisexual men and their wives led by Dr. Eli Coleman of the Program in Human Sexuality at the University of Minnesota. They seemed self-aware and comfortable with group process.

I felt green on both counts. I came from a family – standard Minnesota issue, with stolid Scandinavian and German roots – where talking personally was considered deviant, akin to whining. My bouts of therapy had been brief, and there I had no recourse but to talk – I was paying for the privilege. Here, talking was the norm, it was what we did. It was awkward at first and I held back. The lingo felt stilted: "How do you feel about that?," "It sounds like you're hurting," "I've been there," "What do you need from us?" I practically choked on saying the words but I couldn't deny their effect: the deepening of trust and disclosure, the release of feeling, the power to move on. I relied on a typical dodge, playing the good listener, but these men were such superb listeners themselves and so genuinely interested, the role was redundant. Two of them were ministers, one was a social worker, another had done heavy-duty gestalt work at Essalen with Franz Perls. Besides, talking was surprisingly easy; shared history made filling in all the blanks unnecessary and created an immediate rapport. Having felt alone all my life with this secret, alien and freakish, suddenly I was surrounded by men who had shared the same isolation, the same longing, the same struggle.

I melted into fellowship. Sometimes a group of us would sit together on the couch, shoulder to shoulder, thigh to thigh, the warmth building and passing from body to body like a surge of electric current. I could follow habit and rein myself in, or relax into the angle of repose. It felt comfortable the first time Jim turned and put his arm around me, then rubbed my back as we talked, a natural extension of our conversational intimacy. Guys would hold hands while they stood and talked. It was a revelation to this refugee from a no-touch zone, to be suddenly awash in affection, to realize that men could take such innocent liberties with each other. Women did it all the time, we said.

Within a year I had gone to bed with four of the guys. It was remarkably easy, no dating or courtship rituals required. With each encounter I learned more about the unspoken history of the group: who was bedding whom, who had bedded whom, who was plotting to bed whom. If jealousies, rivalries or hurt feelings simmered beneath the surface, they were neither evident nor discussed in group. When Jim and I started being sexual, I looked to him as the more seasoned member of the group to say something during check-in, and when he didn't, I felt we had betrayed the group. The hypocrisy! For a time the Puritan in me wanted it all out in the open, every last affair! Even the group's name was a sham, a cover; we hardly ever talked about our kids. But prudence and self-interest prevailed, and truth was, the backstage sex didn't skew group dynamics. Guys continued to speak candidly about their struggles with identity, coming out, dating and custody; or if they were determined to stay married, getting their wives to understand and accept their sexuality, perhaps the possibility of sex outside the marriage, or excluding that, finding some way to honor the integrity of their gay feelings within the marriage, even if that meant celibacy. The choices were rarely easy; guys agonized, muddled through, hedged from month to month. Through it all we were there for each other, listening and responding, sharing our experience and insight.

I suspect that the sex wasn't an issue for us partly because of the nature of male psychology. A certain matter-of-factness prevailed in these affairs; the sex could be playful, experimental, negotiated. Many of the men were protective of their marriages, and they were probably even more adept than most males at compartmentalizing feelings and behavior. Generally, they were mature, direct in communication and able to resolve conflicts practically, one-on-one. If anything, the sex probably strengthened the group, deepening the bonds of trust, affection and affinity that held us together, as it did in the armies and academies of ancient Greece.

After a couple of hot sessions with Jim – making love was a frantic scrambling over every last inch of each other's terrain, a discovery that the body, in its infinitely subtle register, could be played like a musical instrument – I started to get attached. He was a fascinating man, twenty years older, a minister conversant with the full spectrum of spirituality, east to west, ancient to new age. He was the first person since my confirmation pastor to acknowledge my spiritual side; I had drifted away from my religious upbringing and had felt unmoored ever since. Yet some glimmer of that fervent boy must have remained in the man now walking beside him, for he named it, with a tone solemn and reverent.

"I don't know why you discount yourself as a spiritual person, Bob. I see you as very spiritual." I flushed with pleasure and surprise, as if he were conferring something on me, but something I already owned outright, but had forgotten – like a second confirmation of my baptism.

When I started to get infatuated, Jim administered a gentle correction by becoming less available. He was committed to his marriage, after his fashion. I was hurt, bewildered, but quickly recovered. These were the rules of the game, after all. The initial heat subsided into a close, comfortable friendship, until one afternoon when I was visiting him at his office and he initiated a heavy make-out session. Then it was my turn to administer the correction and redefine my comfort zone until the friendship stabilized again.

After Jim came Ed – via Daniel, that is, whom I had met outside the group. When our "affairlet" sputtered out – this was a brave new world indeed, where a passion could spread with the intensity of a wildfire, consuming the very oxygen it needed to sustain itself– I rebounded into the waiting arms of Ed, who was trying to negotiate an open marriage with his wife. Both group members, we agreed for reasons of mutual convenience to be "sex buddies," meeting at my place every Wednesday evening for three months. Ed liked regularity. It was fun and uncomplicated, just what the doctor ordered – for me, that is; this time it was Ed's turn to get attached. When he proposed bringing me home to meet the Misses, I bolted. It took several angry phone conversations to salvage the friendship. He later supported me through my breakup with my partner of three years, I supported him as he addressed a history of sexual abuse as a child, and together we worked on various projects in the gay community, organizing protests, screening political candidates and creating a conference celebrating alternative family life-styles.

And that's the way it was in the Fathers' Group. We had our affairs, and we settled them, and out of that sometimes tempestuous process rich friendships born. What mattered was the group – it was all in the family, so to speak. A core of us stayed together for several years; I had never known such fellowship. Some men left, others joined, some drifted in only for a meeting or two, others arrived in crisis, homeless, jobless. Frank had lost his marriage, medical practice and license, had been arrested and exposed in the papers and been forced to relocate because of sexual behavior with a minor patient. He had to rebuild his life from the ground up. We were there for him, complete with a place to stay. Earl, the man who nursed his wife and came out at age sixty-five, had a lovely home near Lake Nokomis that he made available to these men in transition. Some stayed a few weeks till they got on their feet again; Frank stayed three years. He and Earl became fast friends.

After twenty-five years of serving hundreds of men, the group survives to this day, self-subsistent, with no affiliation or outside support and minimal structure. It exists because the need exists. It has undergone several organizational crises, almost folding twice, but each time it has been rescued. While all the original members are long gone, there's a generational continuity, a group of "elders" who stay on long enough to ensure that the next cadre can carry on the work. They know that if the group dies, it will only have to be reinvented.

I marvel at what this pack of "lone wolves" has done – how, solitary creatures that we sometimes are, we have taken such good care of each other. I marvel too at this dynamic interplay of sex and friendship, how bonds of affection and fellowship have been strengthened, and how creatures so skittish of intimacy have managed to form such a wealth of close attachments within relatively loose affiliations. Is this a gift of men?

As I said, I was lucky. I came out into a ready-made family. I got to explore sex and friendship in a safe, positive environment. The opportunity I missed in adolescence – to learn how to integrate tender and sexual feelings while developing meaningful relationships – I found in part in the Fathers' Group.

I didn't always behave admirably. Inside and outside the group I was a relentless serial monogamist. I sometimes wondered if my compatriots who prowled the bath-houses and beaches at night didn't demonstrate more honesty and integrity in their "wordless encounters"; they didn't cloak their predations with the fig leaf of relationship. But language gets loaded around sex. Inexperienced and confused, often what I was seeking, what I needed, was closeness, and sex was an efficient way to break down the barriers between men. Also, given the urgency of male sex, you sometimes had to get it out of the way to get on with the business of friendship, where it could prove a powerful bond. If the craving upon going to bed was more to get a pizza and talk politics, that issue was settled.

I boasted in my second or third year of coming out that I was intimate friends with eleven men. Sex might have been involved at one point in some of these relationships, but by then I was comfortable forming nonsexual friendships with men, and the gay issue and the energy it generated provided a ready entree. What I meant by "intimate friends" was precise: at any given time I knew where they were and what they were doing, how they were feeling, what issues they were facing. This took tremendous time and energy and had a driven quality to it. I was making up for lost time – all those boys I never knew.

I can step back and analyze myself, and as always, the truth is multi-faceted and elusive, but my memories of this time are hallowed. For all my ravenous, rapacious hunger to know so many men –there's that language again – I met each of these men with an openness, a genuine interest, a generosity of spirit and a willingness to suspend judgment and take him on his own terms. Many of these men remained friends for years, some of them to this day.

When I first came out my father had trouble accepting it. Two or three times he spewed venomous invective at me; he was drinking heavily at the time. I could talk easily with Mom about my gay life, my friends or who I was dating, but I wondered how to keep Dad apprised; The issue was such a flashpoint between us. Once you've come out, made the basic statement, how do you keep the subject alive in the other person's mind so they can begin to accept it? My strategy was to tell him about the men in the Fathers' Group. But for one fact, they were men like himself, educated, professional, family men, with interesting backgrounds, personalities and opinions. So I told him stories about them and their lives; it seemed to be the ground where we could meet. He listened, he got to know them, and through them, me.

Three years into my coming out he surprised me by handing me his latest copy of *Mother Jones*, which was running a series on modern love. The subject THAT month was gay love and he thought I might be interested. The article by Edmund White drew on a contrast between two trees. Heterosexual love, White wrote, was like an oak tree that sent one tap root deep into the earth, which gave the tree its stability; homosexual love, by contrast, was like the banyan tree which drops innumerable roots down from its branches and can spread hundreds and hundreds of feet in diameter. It is no less stable even though its roots are lightly tethered to the earth. He was characterizing the multiplicity and fluidity of gay relationships that segue back and forth between sex and friendship.

After finishing it, I called Dad back excitedly. "That's a terrific article, Dad. What did you think of it?"

"I don't know. It's beyond my ken."

"Yeah, I know what you mean. I wouldn't have imagined such a world was possible either, before I came out, but that's the way it is."

I liked it that my dad suspended his judgment. I knew that he had made his peace with my decision, even though he never spoke of the matter with me again. That was the way in our family. This new family that I was lucky enough to have stumbled into, it operated by a different set of rules entirely, yet for all its fluidity and mutability, its lightly tethered roots, it was no less nurturing and supportive, no less real and present for me.

Classic Dream

In my second year of coming out I reported a disturbing dream to a therapist. I was dating a man and though I cared for him deeply and felt attracted, I couldn't come to climax with him. Often I could barely feel him taking me in his hand or mouth. This was the primary problem being addressed in therapy but of course it was only the tip of the iceberg; most of the talk was about what lay beneath the waters.

In the dream I am sitting cross-legged in the alley behind our house on Quail, where I grew up, idly poking at cinders with a stick. I hear derisive laughter and look up to see a figure standing on the fire escape of a building across the way. It's my ex-wife, or wait, it's my boyfriend – no, he's standing just behind her. The figures blur and separate and merge again. The mocking laughter is Judy's. She's throwing me something, tossing back something I've given to her, and as I track its arc high in the sky, I realize to my horror that it's my severed scrotum.

Doug sits opposite me, cool and unflappable as always, smartly dressed, firmly toned, his dark moustache crisply trimmed, taking notes and saying nothing.

I watch the sac spin wildly through the air, flopping end over end, and feel frantic that my testicles will spill out and be lost to me forever. The laughter intensifies to a shriek and my face burns with shame. "What have I done, what have I done?," I think to myself.

"I know why she's laughing," I tell Doug. "A couple of years before the marriage ended, I had a vasectomy. Judy and I were hardly having sex at all – I was in the middle of the worst depression of my life – but I had a vasectomy so she wouldn't have to keep taking the pill. It was a grand, empty, self-sacrificial act. I can still hear the metallic snip of those scissors. What a fucking joke!"

"What's the joke?," he asks.

"My marriage, my whole life." More silence, more scribbling.

By the time the sac lands in my lap, I'm relieved to discover it's neatly sewn up like a coin purse, testicles intact. In the next scene of the dream I am on a quest, going from house to house, milling through crowds of strange men at one party after another. I am excited, bewildered and lost, trying to find someone or something, I'm not sure what. At the last house I receive a call from my father.

"Go home, your house is in ruins," he says matter-of-factly.

I hurry home to find our Fifties-style rambler apparently intact, nestled snugly under the spreading oak that shades the broad sloping lawn. On entering, however, I'm shocked to find the interior totally gutted – not a stick of furniture, the windows stark, the walls stripped to the studs, the rafters gaping overhead. All that remains is a mirror inside the entry way. I look and I'm sweating blood, oozing red from every pore; I shake my head and look again, and this time I watch myself decompose like a corpse, the images flashing before my eyes in stop-action photography, the flesh rotting and peeling back from my bones.

"That's it, then I wake up." Doug is scribbling furiously now. I imagine him rushing into print as soon as the session is over.

"Wow, that's some dream," he says as he finishes. "What do you think it means, what did you feel afterwards?"

"Despair," I say. "The ridiculous, utter folly of it all, my grand hollow gesture, the whole marriage. I sacrificed my sexuality, and for what? Judy didn't even desire me, and there I was, grimly striving year after year to make something work that was inherently impossible. How do I even begin to make up for what I've lost?" My eyes fill with tears.

"Well, Bob, look at it this way, you got your balls back, didn't you?" I laugh. Doug has a practical wisdom, a way of putting things into perspective. "I think it's a classic coming-out dream," he continues, and with his gentle coaching, I begin to find in the shifting, shimmering nuance of the dream's details, what lies just the other side of despair: hope. I see the man-boy playing in the alley, my boyfriend like a guardian angel standing watch on the fire escape, my home cleanly stripped and ready for one helluva remodeling job, and my bones spanking clean, ready for new life. It's all of a piece, this life of mine. I will put on the new man; I will take as my own this glorious adventure of discovery, uncharted, unauthorized, heady with risk and promise, with no guarantee of an outcome, no seal of approval from any authority other than my own.

In our dozen or so sessions Doug and I do not solve the problem of my not climaxing – that's for later. What he gives me is an openness to the adventure, a flowing with what it has to teach me.

"Isn't it rich?," he says during one particularly fruitful session, looking up from his notes to comment on the sea of issues bubbling just below the surface. Rich indeed, this mix of grieving, shame, ingrained tricks of mind, mistrust of the body and sex itself, the fear of moving forward and embracing an unknown future – all the impediments to my being present in the moment, any moment, not just the sexual moment. In my coming out, I am mapping whole new circuits of thinking and feeling, learning how to integrate fantasy and reality, tenderness and desire. I am learning to cope with the impetuosity of the male sex drive, dealing with the problem of getting sexual too quickly, then playing catch-up with my feelings and addressing issues of trust after the fact. I am learning, belatedly, to like men; I have desired them from afar, now I am learning to like them up close. All these issues and more I am confronting clumsily, in a kind of delayed adolescence, without rules or rituals or role models to guide me... and everything, like the least shift of a lover's weight, registers in bed.

"No wonder you have trouble coming," he says. Doug gives me permission, and confidence, to trust myself and improvise. He is one of the first fully out, well-adjusted gay men I have met, and he tells me enough about himself that I have a sense of where this life of mine might lead. Not to back-alley sex, alcoholic stupor, mindless hedonism, hysterical self-caricature or a lonely old age – what I have feared from the dark picture painted by the mainstream culture – but a life of purpose and character. But I, a mostly conventional man, will have to write my own script.

"My lover and I have been together ten years now," Doug tells me one day when I am confessing my fears about charting these waters. "We never expected that or planned on it, it just happened, negotiated a day at a time."

At the close of the session when I report my dream, Doug and I stand for our ritual handshake. It's an elegant space where we do this work, decorated in tasteful grays and whites, raised a step from the rest of the office and set off by two white round wooden pillars – a sanctuary of sorts. On the wall behind him is a print by M.C. Escher I have noted countless times before, but never really seen till now. A hand holding a pencil is drawing on a piece of paper another hand holding a pencil. The two pencil points converge, forming an endless loop in one of those curious Escher puzzles: where does the action begin and end, what is reality and what is dream or intention, who is the drawer and who is the drawn?

"Is that about therapy?," I ask, thinking of the act of self-creation embedded in the act of self-understanding – the authoring of one's own being.

He smiles. "In all my years of practice, you're the first client who's ever seen the connection."

Thinking back now, after all these years, as embedded as I am in the writing of this memoir, I think the drawing describes that process as well. I am writing, and I am written; I tell my story, and my story tells me. It's an endless loop, this act of living and re-membering.

Embracing the Exile

At a men's gathering ten years after I came out, I had one of those experiences all too common for gay people in this culture – a discounting of my identity and place in the world – and for a moment I was pitched into primal anxiety.

The poet Robert Bly and storyteller Michael Mead were leading a Friday evening session with both men and women present, prior to a men-only gathering on Saturday. They traded stories, recited poems, sang and drummed to a packed crowd in a church basement, all in celebration of the mythic roots of the great cosmic dance between the sexes, that mysterious dynamic of attraction and repulsion between male and female that lies near the heart of creation and drives so much of song and story.

I sat in the front row, enthralled like the rest of the audience, but soon grew uneasy. I was single, gay and recently separated from my partner of three years. This was a roomful of smiling, laughing heterosexual couples whose unions had the sanction of law and custom, and now were being cloaked in the mantle of myth and magic.

I grew anxious as I approached that all-too-familiar abyss of shame and meaninglessness never far from consciousness. Where did I fit into this cosmic dance of creation? Was I, and the way I loved, merely a cultural anomaly? I felt alien and alone.

Bly's wit was barbed and wise; the younger Mead, boyish and clever, whose head and torso bobbed and jerked to the driving rhythm of his drum, was a warm and mellow counterpoint to the grey-maned curmudgeon. I couldn't help being drawn into their good-humored fellowship, and soon found myself caught up in the spell of sound and story... and the more generous truths of art.

Like many gay men, I had been married. I had known heterosexual privilege first-hand. I knew that, as husband and father, with the credentials of marriage and family behind me, I enjoyed a blanket legitimacy. I fit in, my life had purpose and meaning, whatever the actual merits of the case. I looked around the room at the smiling couples, observed their knowing glances, the easy touch, felt the electricity in the air. I knew the truth, however. Beneath the façade of solid couple-fronts lay the fragility of intimacy negotiated day-by –day out of the tender hopes and dreams, the fears and disappointments of everyday life. Beneath the legends and tales, the sanctifying embrace of the one great myth, lay the actual stories of the people in this room.

Having experienced both worlds first-hand, I knew that my union with my male partner, despite its imperfections, had been as significant as any in that room; for me as a gay man who had made a clumsy and hurtful compromise with conventional marriage, it was far more genuine and fulfilling. I was engaged with my male lover – body, mind, heart and spirit – to a degree I could never have achieved with a woman. My gay relationship had all the magic and mystery, the power and passion of any heterosexual union.

Where were the stories and songs, however, and how did I and the way I loved fit into the great dance of creation? An insight came. Yes, we gay people are a people of exile. We don't belong. Yet the ironic fact is that many celebrations of the great dance between the sexes were probably created by shamans, poets and artists who themselves occupied the margins of conventional society. They drew power from that ambiguous position and were able to create, explore and push the boundaries of the possible because of their freedom from rigid roles and cultural expectations. In our exile, we gay people have a peculiar gift: the ability to step outside the given and see the world from a different slant.

Bly and Mead continued to weave their tapestry of song and legend – the marriage of Sky and Earth, the creation of the Mud People, the tales of the Monkey God and Adam and Eve. But in the more generous and universal way of art, these stories spoke to a deeper truth: our human craving for union, and the transformative power of the encounter with the Other. My engagement with my male partner, with its own struggles and transformations, was part of this larger story. Sex and Gender are only two ways of imagining it. Any tale of encounter – whether focused on differences in race, age, class, ethnicity, species or simply the meeting with the Stranger – is at its deepest level about aloneness, the craving for union, the shattering of the ego and finally, the necessary repair of the tattered fabric of Creation. The Jews have a word for this: *tikkun*.

Was this rationalization? Where were our off-spring, how did we people and renew the earth? For this is what creation myths are about. Well, I had a daughter, didn't I, and I wasn't alone in this, and many gay couples had adopted or were having children by any means possible. We were re-inventing and expanding the very notion of family itself. Furthermore, in our role as ministers, teachers, counselors, social workers, mentors, "uncles" and "aunts" to the young – all vocations to which we have been historically called – we nurtured, fathered and mothered countless souls and psyches. Also, as writers, painters, sculptors, architects, actors, musicians, and designers of interiors, hair, fashion and style, we had given birth to countless forms of truth and beauty. The world was the richer for our progeny.

The next morning, refreshed and renewed – I want to say "re-paired" -- I gathered with the men in the low-ceilinged lunchroom of Plymouth Congregational Church on the edge of downtown Minneapolis. I had never been among so many men. The quarters were close and hot, our bodies milled and touched, the room was aromatic with sweat, tongues and musk, and in the low rumblings and muted roar, the swelling tide of male conversation, the room was electric with masculine energy. I assumed that most of these men were heterosexual, but I felt no estrangement. I belonged.

Briefed on the day's events, we filed upstairs to wait our turn in the morning's initiation rite: a long crawl on our elbows and bellies over the matted straw lining the makeshift tunnel, which was draped with sheets and blankets, that led into the darkened auditorium. There was a time, and not too long ago, when I would have shrunk from such an experience, viewed it as hokey and pretentious, but not now. I knew the place I was called to enter. It had become familiar ground, that sure, steady place inside, so hard-won through all these years of struggle, to which my whole life had led. When I emerged into the thunderous cavern and heard the whoops and yells, the songs and drumming of my brothers who lined the walls, I knew that I, and the way I loved, were as much a part of the age-old human story as any man who ever walked the earth.

Author's note: *Embracing the Exile* is the title of a book by John Fortunato.

GIFTS

God's Joke

I'm walking up this path that winds round and round the mountain. I have two friends with me, Crazy Bob and The Editor. I don't like the editor much – in my sessions he sits stiff and stern in his chair, watching my every move, passing judgment and making his pronouncements – but frankly, Crazy Bob isn't much better. He's a nut-case, ferocious, immature. I'm stuck with them, however; they're part of me, and we're on our way to the top of the mountain where I'm supposed to meet this Wisdom Figure who's got a gift for me.

How do I get myself into these things? My so-called friends are aspects of my personality that have surfaced in therapy, and I've spent the past two months in dialog with them, learning who they are and how they drive my behavior. I may have come into counseling with a manageable problem, but I'll be lucky to escape with anything short of a multiple personality disorder.

The problem is this. Four years after coming out I found the man of my dreams. We clicked right away, the sex was incredible and all the pieces fell into place, but now, after two years of living together, we're quarreling and our fights last for weeks. He's got this close woman friend who goes back seventeen years; they were in the Christian commune movement together in the Seventies, then raised forty foster kids as a business. He's always there for her, from providing a shoulder to cry on at any hour of the night, to fixing her toilet. They sometimes talk two or three times a day on the phone. She won't let go, he won't set limits and I've repressed my jealousy and resentment so long, thinking them ignoble and feeling I should honor their friendship, I'm lashing out, unable to negotiate reasonable compromises. I can't sleep; the thought that keeps running through my mind is, "You've made your bed, now lie in it." How could this be happening? Is everything a joke?

My mountain walk is not a dream exactly, it's a waking dream, a guided meditation facilitated by my therapist, who works within the framework of psychosynthesis. I go into these sessions self-conscious and suspicious, not even sure I believe in what I'm doing, but Paul gets me to relax and work with whatever my subconscious throws me, even my resistance. Eventually the flow of imagery and the mind's story-telling impulse take over, and I usually surprise myself.

When my friends and I get near the top of the mountain – after lame attempts at conversation – Paul asks if I see the Wisdom Figure. What pops into my head is Michelangelo's God from the Sistine Chapel ceiling, flying through the sky with his grey beard and flowing blue robes. I lament my lack of originality and am almost too embarrassed to report it to Paul – this session will be a bust.

By the time he lands, however, the figure is transformed. It's Walt Whitman sauntering toward me, dressed in a country motley with a broad leather hat, his grey mane and beard sprouting tiny flowers and field-grasses – or are those bees buzzing round his beard, as if he himself is the flower? He looks rosy, refreshed, as if he's just risen from a nap in the meadow, or maybe a roll in the hay. He's leaning toward me as he approaches, with a mischievous twinkle in his eyes, his arms behind his back. He's got something for me. He whips it out and it's a giant red phallus.

"Know, accept, enjoy!," he says.

What a gift. Not once in my life have I ever been equal to the full glory of it, but my whole life is an effort to rise to the occasion, so to speak. From the acceptance of my sexuality have flowed countless other gifts: an open-ness to life, a trusting to its deeper currents, a sense of awakening and adventure, increased empathy, love, friendship, creativity, spirituality.

What a joke – that so much of who we are as human beings is bound up with something so base and visceral as sex. Our dreams, ideals, passions, loves and attachments; our impossible strivings and heroic efforts; all the accomplishments of our indomitable spirit – yoked to this body that shits, fucks and rots. What an unholy marriage, what a colossal, glorious joke.

Owning

I didn't save my relationship – does therapy ever solve a problem? It gives clarity, helps to heal, lays the seeds and tills the soil for future growth. I didn't stay stuck in an impossible situation, however, I didn't internalize the failure and stigmatize myself, and I took responsibility for my part in the breakdown. I owned the passive people-pleaser so greedy for approval that he betrayed his own vital interests. Also, I emerged from that relationship with an important truth about myself that no amount of failure could erase: I could love, I could love as other people loved, with my whole heart and soul.

For eight months after my partner and I split, every Friday night I attended a gay Adult Children of Alcoholics meeting, even though I often felt uncomfortable there and wondered if I was wasting my time. Who were these strangers anyway? They dropped in and out inexplicably, they told stories that were painful and hard to follow, some of them wallowed in their victimhood, still blaming their parents after all these years for everything that had gone wrong with their lives. What a sorry lot of whiners and losers, I thought.

Often during those early weeks and months I came close to quitting the group. One guy in particular stands out from that time, a refugee from an Emotions Anonymous group, a blimp of a man who seemed with every movement in danger of slipping loose from his moorings. What spilled out of him during an interminable check-in was a word salad of grief, sobs and words, sighs, catches and moans, tossed together indiscriminately, with no facts, context or syntax to give them meaning – raw, unparseable pain. I wanted to run from the room.

But I belonged here, somehow I knew that. I was one of them, the adult child of an alcoholic, a background that abetted my incompetence in asserting myself constructively in intimate relationships. I swallowed my pride, suspended my doubts about the cultishness of twelve-stepping, and shared my story, dropped it into the communal pool where it lost some of its solitary edge and seemed both less and more as it merged with the other stories. We were a made-to-order community every Friday night, no matter who showed, bound together by our common need, the framework of the program, the trust of complete confidentiality and a spirit of unconditional acceptance. I was amazed at the wisdom and empathy that flashed forth in these gatherings. If I missed something, someone else caught it; if I couldn't connect, someone else could. Collectively we were inspired, possessing a power beyond the sum of our parts.

I had come into the group with the express purpose of letting go of the relationship and learning to advocate more effectively for myself, but I left with much more. I learned first-hand the power of humility, trust, community and intentionality – choosing to focus energy purposefully toward the accomplishment of concrete goals. I could make of the group whatever I chose, and it would give me whatever I sought, as long as I knew what I wanted.

Demonstrated for me once again was the transformative power of owning my life. Coming out didn't end my problems, and it created a host of new ones, but the difference was, I had a commitment to this life, it expressed me and had meaning for me. Every difficulty, therefore, was transformed into a learning opportunity, another step along the way; and embracing it, I turned it to my advantage.

Knowing

    I seem to have this knack for knowing what I need to do. For all my resistance and confusion, I usually stumble onto the right path. My story since coming out is a tale of remarkable, almost blessed serendipity. A life turned upside-down, that was never right in the first place, has been righting itself ever since, as if by an energy uncoiling inside itself.

    Take friendship, for example. From adolescence through my mid-thirties, I was this odd, almost reclusive figure, uncomfortable and mistrustful regarding people generally, but men especially. I have since discovered a talent for friendship, and a hidden, I might even say occult, truth: whether in the form of casual sex that led to life-long friendships, or friendships that led to a deepening of political activism or spiritual awareness thanks to an infusion of sexual energy, or the sum total of all my encounters with men, enlivened by that same erotic energy, which taught me that I could like as well as love my own sex – the synergy of sex and friendship has been a driving force in my life. That was readily apparent on my fiftieth birthday as I looked around the room at the dozen guys I had invited to the party, all close friends – I had been sexual with most of them. Nothing in my prior life, with its tidy rules and comfortable compartments, could have prepared me for this abundance of freedom, and the only way through it was to follow the energy wherever it led.

Early in the process of coming out, I picked a poem as my oracle, or it picked me – it's hard to know how to phrase these things. Not in all the years since, not with all my literary training, have I ever fully understood the words of this poem, yet they speak to me, like music, they speak to me beyond my understanding. And as my life unfolds, my comprehension grows. The poem is "The Waking" by Theodore Roethke and it begins:

> I wake to sleep, and take my waking slow.
> I feel my fate in what I cannot fear.
> I learn by going where I have to go.

This sense of feeling my way through life, as if life were a kind of waking dream, trusting to what it has to teach me, and learning as I go – that is the spirit of my coming out. For every misstep and disappointment, for all my foolishness and ferocity, this trust has never failed me. Every mishap takes me to another level of insight and growth.

> I feel my fate in what I cannot fear.

This is so different from how I used to live, so watchful and on guard, bristling with an arsenal of explanations, justifications and excuses. It's as if a curtain divides the two halves of my life – a waking if you will, but a waking into a different kind of consciousness. I am always keenly aware that I am only half-aware, and ever open to what the next moment has to teach me. I am in this life, and of it. I am not the watcher, but the witness.

Cauchemar

In 1990, in my forty-ninth year, I had a crisis. My vision loss, genetic in origin, had progressed gradually enough till then to allow me to make needed adjustments along the way, but the pace was quickening and my patchwork of accommodations was unraveling. I was getting lost in familiar places, bumping into colleagues at work, drifting out into busy intersections while crossing streets, and I could no longer read without the aid of a closed-circuit TV. From the onset of the disease, night blindness in adolescence, through the ever-narrowing tunnel vision of my twenties, thirties and forties, as my retinas continued to degenerate, I had held out hope that a small island of clear vision would remain, enough for me to read, navigate, continue work and appreciate beauty. I would get no last-minute reprieve, however, and what I had thought would never happen to me was finally happening – I was going totally blind.

I was pitched into depression, and not all the stratagems that had worked so well throughout the decade of my coming out – meditation, journaling, self-analysis and talking to friends – could lift me out of it. I had begun to think myself almost immune; after all, I finally knew who I was and where I stood, and could no longer get lost in the Fun House, trapped in that endless maze of self-questioning.

During this period, I had a night visitor. For months my sleep had been agitated; I'd lie awake for hours, my mind and heart racing. On one of those nights I awoke to the sound of rushing air in the hallway outside my bedroom door. Whoosh, whoosh, back and forth, like a child was running loose in the apartment. I could hear the thudding of the feet, feel the shaking of the floor, of my bed! This is crazy, I thought, I'm hallucinating – it's just the pounding of my own heart. Then someone was in the room with me – I knew this as surely as I knew the limits of my own skin. I could hear and sense his breathing, his footsteps as he neared the bed, feel the slight depression as he placed his hand on the edge of the mattress. Why couldn't I open my eyes? I was paralyzed with fear. Maybe, I thought, if I lie still enough, pretending I'm asleep, it will go away – it's only a bad dream. Whoosh, whoosh. He was circling the bed now, left to right, right to left and back again, faster and faster. I could feel the wind in the room. By sheer force of will I forced myself upright to face my intruder. He was a tall, lean young man about nineteen or so, naked, with a blank look in his eyes. He bobbed and weaved wildly around the perimeter of my bed, like a caged animal desperate to get out – only he wanted in! I tried to scream but couldn't.

I knew immediately who it was. Crazy Bob. When I had first encountered him in therapy with Paul three years earlier, he was a boy of about eight or nine cowering with his back to me in the corner of a dark cell. I could barely make him out as he shivered, frail and naked, rocking back and forth on his haunches.

"Approach him," Paul had said. I held back. "Go up to him, see what he does." Paul's method was to use guided visualization to get me to manifest aspects of my personality and engage with them, the goal being to gain greater understanding of how they drove my behavior and, ultimately, to achieve integration of the self.

I came nearer. "Say something to him," Paul said. I felt tongue-tied.

"What do you need from me?," I said as I took another step toward him. He turned his head and snarled and snapped, his eyes wild and full of betrayal. That was the beginning of what can only be termed an uneasy acquaintance, the first step in a long process of reclamation that was interrupted as the immediate crisis, the dissolution of my relationship, pressed to the fore. That process continues to this day.

Now here he was again. I may have forgotten him in the interim but clearly he had his own life. I was terrified. I crawled under the covers and felt him come over to the side of the bed and stand there. Go away, go away, I thought, I can't deal with you right now, too much is going on with me. I renounced him with everything I had but he wouldn't budge; he wanted to crawl into bed with me. "GO AWAY!" – did I shout it or think it? – but then a different energy took hold, and I began to get aroused. I let him in, and as he drew closer I felt a shudder begin throughout my body, and I got scared. Thoughts of possession and stories I remembered from Llewellyn about people whose souls left their bodies, only to find those bodies occupied and unavailable for return later flashed through my mind. "No, no," I said, and the shuddering stopped. He was gone.

The next night I asked my daughter to stay with me in case he returned, and when he did I somehow managed to let out a scream and she came running into the room. Again, he was gone. I related the experience to a friend of mine versed in the occult who told me it was probably a *cauchemar* – a recurring nightmare that includes a visitor, often with sexual overtones – and gave me a spell to ward it off. The third night I placed a dish of water on my nightstand with an open scissors behind it, the blades pointing toward the bedroom door, and that was the last of my night visitor.

In my mind I struck a bargain with him: don't come at night any more and I'll go back into therapy to deal with you. But the heat was off and my engagement with the therapeutic process was half-hearted, smacking more of appeasement than anything else, and the energy quickly dissipated. I have to admit, however, that I wrote some powerful poetry during that time, with a fresh voice and full of raucous rhythms.

To this day, I sometimes wonder, what would have happened if I had gone all the way with him?

Living in the Body

After I split with my partner of three years, I was a wounded animal; I needed a constructive outlet for my grief. Then in 1989 the Minnesota AIDS Massage Project opened its doors to people who were non-certified, providing a short training course to bring them up to speed, because the need for massage was so great. It was the height of the AIDS crisis and I was bawling at the news most evenings, feeling powerless. I loved to touch and had good hands, and here I was newly singled and deprived of a touch object.

It seemed a perfect fit. I had been doing volunteer publicity, board work and public speaking for a variety of gay causes, but these activities drew on established strengths; I wanted to develop in a different direction, do something physical, mindless and one-on-one, cultivating underdeveloped areas: intuition, emotion and empathy. Something deeper would be tapped, however: spirituality. It was another of those serendipitous decisions of mine.

I did this work for fourteen years at the Aliveness Project in Minneapolis, a drop-in center for people with

HIV/AIDS, usually two massages a week, and gained far more than I ever gave. Sometimes a man would ask me afterwards, "I know what I get out of this but what's in it for you?"

My short answer was, "I get a good workout, I get really relaxed, and no matter how grumpy or achy or blue I feel when I begin, I almost always end revitalized. It's like stepping into the water for a swim – I emerge refreshed and renewed." True, as far as it went.

Massage is like meditation for me; it concentrates and integrates mind, body and spirit. I can come into it with a turmoil of emotions. Initially I may not like the person on the table – their personality, smell, the texture of their skin. In the context of disease I can be repelled by the body's gross physicality, as it lies naked like a cadaver on the table; I shrink from mortality like a swimmer feeling the ragged pull of rip-tide out to sea. Then there's the issue of arousal. If a man is well-built, my fingers act as my eyes – my field of vision has become so narrow I can't see whole bodies any more – and like a starved man I experience afresh the beauty I can no longer see, sometimes with stirrings of desire.

My remedy for all of this is to stay with the body. I plant my feet squarely on the floor and begin my *effleurage* with long flowing strokes up the back, paying attention to my breathing and technique, going through the steps of my routine. Touch, smell, movement, the sound and feel of the body yielding, the breath deepening – every sense is engaged as flesh warms to flesh and my feet do a rhythmic dance, criss-crossing from side to side, head to toe and back again. I am led out of myself and experience something of the essence of another – their stories, humor, sadness, courage, struggles and silence.

Subjecting myself to this steady, gentle discipline composes my soul, brings into harmony the fitful chaos of the self. A mysterious exchange of energy occurs, and sometimes I lose myself and become one with the dance of massage, entering another realm of being altogether, the sacred ground of healing where giver and receiver are restored.

My work at the Aliveness Project fit me like a glove. There, every week, in a shuttered, ramshackle room filled with the clutter of healing paraphernalia – chiropractic and massage tables, privacy screens, piles of linens and pillows, bolsters and blankets, trays laden with oils and lotions, and sometimes lingering in the air the pungent scent of burnt sage – I could address my grief, fear and loneliness, satisfy my craving for touch, remedy a certain atrophy of personality and become whole in the act of healing another.

Were my motives mixed? As mixed as my humanity – a tangle of impulses base, practical, selfless and sublime. It is the marvel of moving through that mix in the dance of massage, passing from fear and self-doubt to acceptance and wholeness, that kept me coming back year after year.

One of my first regular clients was Robb, a man in the last stages of AIDS. For almost a year before he died, he came every Wednesday afternoon, even toward the end when he had to hobble in on two canes and be helped up onto the table. I ministered to his body, he ministered to my spirit. His stories and quiet courage, his gentle humor, his total acceptance of his dying, while at the same time fully affirming whatever life was left to him, moved me.

One day as I was getting the room ready for him –

turning on the space heater, putting the sheets on the table – I flashed to a memory of myself as a little boy of five swabbing my father's naked feet with Vicks Vaporub and wrapping them tenderly in long streamers of toilet paper to soothe painful corns on the balls of his feet. I had done this several times and it was a familiar memory, but for the first time I placed it, in the house on 3rd Street, where we lived just after he returned from the war, a separation of nearly two years that by all accounts was awkward and painful for both of us. What patience he must have had to endure this messy ritual of repatriation. Then I recalled that, until I was twelve, I had wanted to be a doctor and had told everyone of my plans. Robb startled me out of my reverie as he entered the room, and suddenly the connection was clear, between the boy of five, the boy of twelve and the man who now got such fulfillment from doing healing work with men. What was I doing but healing myself?

It is partial, this healing energy in me. I give massage to women also, and I am good at it and like doing it, but it doesn't move me in the same way. The difference is more than sex, the feel of a man's body, though that's part of it. A man lying there in his naked vulnerability, trusting to my hands, speaks to that tender part of me, touches me to the quick.

I think of that magical dream from almost before memory, of my quest to find and heal my uncle in a land far away, my talisman on this life journey.

Spirituality

For me coming out coincides with the recovery of my spirituality. As an adult I denied that every bit as much as my sexuality; freeing the one freed the other.

A power, a life-force was released that flows through and transforms every part of my existence. When I celebrated the tenth anniversary of my coming out, I knew the major work of accepting my sexuality and creating a new life around it was done. What remained was doing the same for my spirituality.

As a child I had a fervent faith, an active sense of the presence of God in the world, but typically, it faded with time. Confirmed a strict Missouri Synod Lutheran, my mother's church, I reacted against its rigidity and drifted into the operative faith of my family, the agnostic secular humanism of my father. That was bolstered by my college experience and the need to fortify a rational, in-control persona to keep the forces of life at bay.

From time to time, however, I would remember those moments in childhood when the face of God broke through ordinary reality, and the awe I felt... and how to explain those rare occasions in adulthood, those unaccountable moments out of time when I sensed the wholeness or greatness of life shining through the skin of everyday experience? A walk by the river, washing dishes, talking with a friend – anything might trigger them. My defense was to dismiss them; I called them "spiritual hiccups" because they didn't make sense, didn't fit my rationalist world-view. Now, after coming out, with no more need to keep life at bay, I know my task: to recover and own this lost spiritual history.

In some sense I have already described my spirituality. It consists not so much of a set of specific beliefs as a faith, an orientation toward life, a trust that if I am open to it, it will teach me what I need to know, take me where I need to go.

For me God is in the moment. If I am open and attentive to the moment, I will know God, and that can happen in a walk or conversation with a friend, in sex, in the act of massage, in writing, in silence, in prayer or reflection. Everything, even my blindness, can be a revelation of God.

A few years ago I wrote a piece, an exercise in my writing group, that captures this faith. The title of it was, "What I would miss if I were dead." My response, which reflects my growing blindness, was as follows.

Rising each morning – each day, crooked and imperfect but full of promise, each broken day splendid in its beginning despite the dismal indictment of the past...

Rising from the warmed sheets, feeling the firm floor under my bare, unsteady feet, finding my balance all over again, scrubbing my face fresh with cold water, the air pungent with the smell of strong coffee. This is a new day!

It is never old, this sense of beginning, and each day, each moment, each breath is full of it.

Everything I do, from straightening my papers to visiting my mother, from calling my friends and making appointments to switching on the radio and hearing Shostakovich or Dylan or some chatter about remembering or forgetting, everything is full of unfolding.

I cannot step outside my door, take a walk or a breath, stroll by the river or through the skyways without some adventure or discovery, some challenge or danger rising to greet me. It can take the form of a stranger, a smell I can't name, a sound once familiar, now alien and tantalizing. Maybe it will take the form of something new I have to learn about moving through a crowd or living in community, as my odd, aloof self is bent every which way in the current of the world. Even the chilly, drizzly air is electric with beauty, danger, excitement – and if I were open to it, I would ride even the whipping winds, which I hate with a passion. My love is imperfect.

Where will my steps take me? Every journey, interior and exterior, from the smallest to the biggest, is full of this question. I may know my destination, my intention, but the getting there is full of mystery, suspense, surprise. Sometimes, in my crabbed moments, I get irritated, frustrated, frightened, so angry I could annihilate the world in a single blast of rage. But just the other side of this chaos is mystery, unfolding; and most of the time I thread that uncertain margin, alive, or nearly alive, to its charge.

Every conversation, every stammering and every flight; every fragrance of spring; the sharp, stark silence of winter air; the ripe decay of autumn – all time, in all its drawing out and dwindling down, is full of beginning.

I can imagine not knowing this. I have been there, sometimes for too long, and no doubt I will visit again. Some people live there and rarely escape this sense of closedness. At any moment I could lose this sense of fullness, and then my life would be one long lament for what I have lost.

I was going to say – when I began this uncertain piece – it is that fullness, that ripeness in every moment, that I would miss if I were dead. But perhaps more accurately, it is that grace that sustains the sense of fullness, that realization larger than myself and my own limited capacity to love and trust and hope, that rolls through me and all things and gives them life – that is what I would miss if I were dead.

And what I would have said, if I had followed out my original thought, is that death is an ending, a slamming shut of the iron door of finality on all possibility.

But if grace, or whatever we choose to name it, is what sustains that sense of fullness, that statement is an absurdity. Grace makes the moment of death, so absolute in its apparent finality, just another beginning, another opening to a greater measure of fullness.

What is the experience of my senses when I am most whole, least broken and separated from creation? It is that sense of opening and unfolding. It is this evidence that I am invited to trust in my times of fear and doubt.

May that grace sustain me even in my darkest moments.

Creativity

It's no accident that my first piece of creative writing, "Arabesque," arose out of a frustrated homosexual experience. And it's no accident that I began creative writing in earnest in my mid-forties when I paired up with my partner of three years and started writing love poetry. The ancients had it right: inspiration is tied to *Eros* and the muses are indispensable agents. Something has to get the juices flowing.

Once given, the gift has to be honored. I have tried to do this, writing most days, taking classes and workshops, being an active member of a writing group for seventeen years, endlessly revising work and pushing limits, and performing countless mercy killings, though never nearly enough. When I first came out I wrote my story – maybe 3,000 words – and showed it to one of the writers in the group, a fine poet. She was kind – we need to be kind to each other about these things. This current effort is far better, though I'm sure I would do it differently a few years hence.

Writing – each piece, each paragraph, each sentence and word – is like that process I describe of living moment to moment, being alive to where each moment takes you. Writing is discovery; I don't know what I think or feel until I put it into words, and the very act of struggling to find those words in their right order advances my awareness and understanding. It's an adventure, an endless loop, like the Escher drawing, like life itself.

Afterword

We like to think of memory as an accurate record, but memory is a story-teller too. It works beneath the surface of consciousness to weave together the raw material of our lives, highlighting some connections while hiding others. It selects, arranges, refines, embellishes, adds, subtracts and recombines, sometimes with a wild imagination all its own. All the while it is telling us our story. It is our only historian, and it is a relentless revisionist.

Don't get me wrong, memory is a record too. For me it preserved intact critical information, as if in a time capsule, for use years later in healing. I have a good memory, vivid, accurate, honest, with a sure sense of chronology. For these reasons I am often a better chronicler of my friends' lives than they are themselves. In this memoir I have been as accurate and honest as possible. But I know that memory plays tricks, memory forgets and memory likes to tell tales. It leads us on and gets us lost in the woods, but if we're attentive to the clues and make the right connections, we can emerge renewed and transformed.

Memory morphs its stories over time. I know this

because I've checked the record, in those few cases where I have copies of letters or journal entries written at the time. What I remember doesn't always tally exactly with the facts, but what I remember is in fact what shaped my sense of my history and identity. Even if I had written my story in real-time, it would have been filled with distortions, omissions and recombinations – the story-telling would have already begun. A year out, five years out, twenty years out... and the story-telling would be continuing, as it did even in the writing of this memoir.

I accept and celebrate the recombinant fluidity of memory. It is part of life and identity, dynamic and evolving, always pressing against the inertia of bare facts, toward meaning. So whenever I can't remember exactly an event or quote or sequence of events, or can't recall precisely what I felt or thought at the time, I know there is little to pin down with any surety. I trust my instincts, my feelings. Sometimes all that remains is a puddle of feeling in the midst of swirling, murky events. I trust that feeling and my response to it, I trust its ability to touch my heart and imagination and lead me where I need to go. Is this story-telling? Yes, it is memory telling me what my life is about, where it's going, where I need to pay attention.

Helping me thread my way through this maze, make the right connections, discern essential patterns, are dreams. It's no accident that many of the chapters of this book revolve around dreams. Like memory, they form the record of that other life of mine, the occult life of the soul. If at times this book has had the feel of an archeological dig, with me sifting through the rubble of my life to make sense of it, to discover its story, dreams lie near the bottom of that dig, closest to bedrock. It's there that I find the shards and relics that give the other fragments shape and meaning.

The soul has its own history. It is mostly hidden, glimpsed at the margins, hinted in highlight and shadow, guessed through dream and memory. We can tell our stories, we can think we live them, bristling with an array of intentions, explanations and excuses, but the truth is, our stories tell us, they tell us who we are, deep down, at the core.

Memory is a heroic act. To try to remember enough of one's life, to see it steady and whole, discerning the basic connections, the patterns and motifs that give it shape and meaning, is to try to stand still in the whirlwind of time and put one's finger to the truth. Has one gone deep enough to catch the essence?

For years I denied a basic truth about myself, that I was gay, yet for all the distortion and the damage that was done, what I see in the pattern of my life is an amazing generosity, a repeated invitation to step into the fullness of my being, whatever my resistance. Lessons and opportunities were offered again and again, the rhythm of renewal never ceased, and dream and memory preserved intact essential information for use years later in healing, when I was finally ready to own who I was.

Generosity – one might almost call it grace. Some people talk of the need to save their souls. My soul saved me. This book has been the story of that rescue.

Acknowledgements

I want to acknowledge the following in the creation of this book: my freshman English teacher and mentor, *Burton J. Weber*, for seeing early on that I had "promise"; teacher *Janet Hagberg*, who planted the seed for this book and validated my sense of writing as a spiritual discipline; friends and writers *Margo Peller Feeley* and *Roger S. Jones*, who believed in me as a writer before I believed in myself; teachers *Jane Brox, Barrie Jean Borich* and *Elizabeth Jarrett Andrew*, for valuable critiquing and workshop experiences; the Loft Literary Center and S.A.S.E/The Write Place, for providing a place where the writing life was honored and nurtured; the McKnight and Jerome Foundations and VSA Arts Minnesota for financial and other assistance; the members of my writing group, the 42nd Street Irregulars, who saw the best and worst of me and never lost faith or patience; the men of the Gay Fathers' group, for being a second family when I first came out, and especially *Earl Stickney*, who nudged me repeatedly to tell this story; *Ruth Benson* (formerly *Randall*), who helped me take myself more seriously; and my partner, *John Schmidt*, who never lets me take myself too seriously – thank heavens – and who is always there for me in that fundamental and life-giving way that only a beloved can be.